ECONOMIC ISSUES, PROBLEMS AND PERSPECTIVES

FEDERAL TAXATION OF WEALTH TRANSFERS

ANALYSES, PROPOSALS AND PERSPECTIVES

ECONOMIC ISSUES, PROBLEMS AND PERSPECTIVES

Additional books in this series can be found on Nova's website under the Series tab.

Additional e-books in this series can be found on Nova's website under the e-book tab.

ECONOMIC ISSUES, PROBLEMS AND PERSPECTIVES

FEDERAL TAXATION OF WEALTH TRANSFERS

ANALYSES, PROPOSALS AND PERSPECTIVES

JERRY WASHINGTON
EDITOR

nova publishers
New York

NOTICE TO THE READER

Library of Congress Cataloging-in-Publication Data

ISBN: 978-1-63482-991-5

Published by Nova Science Publishers, Inc. † New York

CONTENTS

PREFACE

This book contains an explanation of the major provisions of the federal estate, gift, and generation-skipping transfer taxes as they apply to transfers in 2014. It provides basic principles regarding the computation of these three transfer taxes. It also provides a history, description, and analysis of the Federal estate, gift, and generation-skipping transfer taxes (also referred to herein as the "wealth transfer taxes"), as well as a description of selected reform proposals.

In: Federal Taxation of Wealth Transfers
Editor: Jerry Washington
ISBN: 978-1-63482-991-5

Chapter 1

THE FEDERAL ESTATE, GIFT, AND GENERATION-SKIPPING TRANSFER TAXES*

Emily M. Lanza

SUMMARY

This report contains an explanation of the major provisions of the federal estate, gift, and generation-skipping transfer taxes as they apply to transfers in 2014. The following discussion provides basic principles regarding the computation of these three transfer taxes.

The federal estate and generation-skipping transfer taxes were resurrected by the Tax Relief, Unemployment Insurance Reauthorization, and Job Creation Act of 2010 (P.L. 111-312) after a hiatus of one year (2010). The American Taxpayer Relief Act of 2012 (ATRA) permanently extended the estate tax rules enacted by the 2010 Act except for the top tax rate, which increased from 35% to 40% for both the estate and gift taxes.

The federal estate tax is a tax levied on the transfer of property at death and measured by the size of the decedent's estate. The tax is computed through a series of adjustments and modifications of a tax base known as the "gross estate." Certain allowable deductions reduce the gross estate to the "taxable estate," to which is then added the total of all lifetime taxable gifts made by the decedent. The tax rates are applied and,

* This is an edited, reformatted and augmented version of a Congressional Research Service publication 95-416, prepared for Members and Committees of Congress, dated June 5, 2014.

after reduction for certain allowable credits, the amount of tax owed by the estate is reached.

The federal gift tax is a tax imposed on all gratuitous transfers of property made during life. The tax seeks to account for transfers of property that would otherwise reduce the estate and accordingly estate tax liability at death. The donor's tax liability of the gift depends upon the value of the "taxable gift." The taxable gift is determined by reducing the gross value of the gift by the available deductions and exclusions.

The unified transfer tax credit is available against both gift and estate tax liability. To the extent this credit is used to offset gift taxes, it is unavailable to offset estate taxes. The Internal Revenue Code refers to the credit as an "applicable exclusion amount," that is, the amount of taxable gifts or estate that the credit would cover. The applicable exclusion amount in 2014 is $5,340,000.

The generation-skipping transfer tax attempts to close a perceived loophole in the estate and gift tax system where property could be transferred to successive generations without intervening estate or gift tax consequences. There are two basic forms of generation-skipping transfers: the indirect skip, where the generation one level below the decedent receives some beneficial interest in the property before the property passes to the generation two or more levels below; and the direct skip, where the property passes directly to the generation two or more levels below the decedent. The generation-skipping transfer tax is imposed at a flat rate of 40% with an available exclusion of $5,340,000. While it is of the same value, this exclusion is separate from the unified transfer tax credit available for the estate and gift taxes.

INTRODUCTION

This report explains the major provisions of the federal estate, gift, and generation-skipping transfer taxes as they apply to transfers in 2014. The enactment of the Economic Growth and Tax Relief Reconciliation Act of 2001 phased out the estate and generation-skipping transfer taxes over a 10-year period, leaving the gift tax as the only federal transfer tax in 2010.[1] The Tax Relief, Unemployment Insurance Reauthorization, and Job Creation Act of 2010 temporarily (through the end of 2012) reinstated the estate and generation-skipping transfer taxes with lower top rates and larger exemptions and reunified the estate and gift taxes.[2] The American Taxpayer Relief Act of 2012 permanently extended the estate tax rules enacted by the 2010 Act except for the top tax rate, which increased from 35% to 40%.[3]

The federal estate and gift taxes are unified as they utilize the same rate structure. Federal estate and gift taxes also share a lifetime transfer credit. For 2014, this unified credit covers an applicable amount of $5,340,000 per individual.

The federal estate, gift, and generation-skipping transfer tax laws are rather lengthy and complex. This report discusses those major Internal Revenue Code (IRC) and Internal Revenue Service (IRS) regulation provisions which play the dominant role in the determination of estate, gift, and generation-skipping transfer tax liability. This discussion relates only to the taxation of United States citizens and resident aliens while different rules apply to the taxation of nonresident alien individuals. For a discussion on transfer taxes for nonresident aliens, see CRS Report R43576, *Estate and Gift Taxes for Nonresident Aliens*, by Emily M. Lanza.

THE FEDERAL ESTATE TAX

The federal estate tax is a tax on the estate of a decedent, levied against and paid by the estate. Contrastingly, the inheritance tax is imposed on and paid by the heirs of the decedent based upon the money or property that they receive. The determination of federal estate tax liability involves a series of adjustments and modifications of a tax base known as the “gross estate.” Certain allowable deductions reduce the gross estate to the “taxable estate.” Then, the total of all lifetime taxable gifts made by the decedent is added to the taxable estate before tax rates are applied. The result is the decedent’s estate tax which, after reduction for certain allowable credits, is the amount of tax paid by the estate. This discussion will divide the federal estate tax into three components: the gross estate, deductions from the gross estate, and computation of the tax, including allowable tax credits.

The Gross Estate: The Federal Estate Tax Base

The gross estate of a decedent includes the value of all property, real or personal, tangible or intangible, wherever situated, in which the decedent owned an interest on the date of the decedent’s death. The gross estate may also include certain interests in property which the decedent had transferred to another person at some time prior to the date of death.[4]

Certain types of property may be included in the decedent's gross estate if specific IRC conditions are met. Proceeds from a life insurance policy on the life of the deceased may qualify as part of the gross estate if either the proceeds are payable to or for the use of the estate's executor, or if the decedent held any "incidents of ownership" in the policy on the date of death or gave away such incidents of ownership within three years of the date of death.[5] An incident of ownership is an economic right in the policy, such as the right to cancel the policy, change the beneficiary, or borrow against its cash surrender value.[6] Similarly, the value of a survivor's annuity payable because of the death of the decedent is included in the decedent's gross estate if the deceased had the right to receive a lifetime annuity under the same contract.[7]

The value of property owned by the decedent jointly with a right of survivorship in another person, other than the decedent's spouse, may also qualify as part of the gross estate. The contribution of money or money's worth of consideration towards the cost of acquiring the property by someone other than the decedent subsequently reduces the contribution of that property to the gross estate.[8] However, only one-half of the value of property owned jointly with a right of survivorship by a decedent and the surviving spouse, regardless of the relative contributions of the decedent and the surviving spouse, may qualify as part of the gross estate.[9]

In a number of instances, the value of a decedent's gross estate encompasses the value of property not owned by the decedent on the date of death.[10] For example, a decedent's gross estate can include the value of lifetime gifts over which the decedent retained a life interest[11] or the power to alter, amend, terminate, or destroy the beneficial enjoyment of the property.[12] Lifetime gifts that do not take effect until the date of death, irrespective of the number of years that have elapsed between the date of the gift and the date of the donor's death, are also included in the donor's gross estate.[13] However, the gross estate does not include property sold during the decedent's lifetime for full and adequate consideration.

The decedent's gross estate also includes all property subject to a general power of appointment held by the decedent on the date of death, even if the decedent died without exercising that power.[14] A power of appointment is a right, held by a person other than the owner of property, to determine who will enjoy the ownership of or benefit of the property. A power of appointment is "general" if it may be exercised by its holder in favor of the holder, the holder's estate, the holder's creditors, or the creditors of the holder's estate. If a power cannot be exercised in favor of these classes of persons, it is not a general power of appointment, regardless of the size of the classes of beneficiaries in whose favor the power can be exercised.[15]

The property and interests included in the decedent's gross estate are valued at their fair market value on the date of death or, if elected by the executor at his/her discretion, the alternate valuation date. The alternate valuation date is the earlier of either the date of distribution or disposition of the property by the estate or the date six months after the date of death.[16] The "fair market value" of property is the price at which the estate property would change hands between a willing buyer and seller.[17] In such a sale, the buyer and seller should not be compelled to buy or sell. Additionally, both parties should have reasonable knowledge of the relevant facts. The fair market value price does not reflect a forced sale price but the sale price in a market in which the item is most commonly sold to the public.[18] The IRS regulations outline valuation rules for certain types of property such as stocks and bonds, family farms, and closely held businesses where the estate must determine the fair market value under specific conditions.[19]

Deductions from the Gross Estate: Reaching the Taxable Estate

A decedent's taxable estate is determined by reducing the gross estate with allowable deductions, including estate administration expenses, certain debts and losses, the amount of qualified transfers to a surviving spouse, charitable bequests, and state death taxes.

The first deduction to which an estate is entitled is for the funeral expenses, administration expenses, claims against the estate, and unpaid mortgages paid by the estate (to the extent not reflected in the reduced value of estate assets). The estate may deduct these payments if they are paid by the estate and are permitted under the laws of the applicable jurisdiction in which the estate is administered.[20] Additionally, the estate may deduct the amount of any casualty or theft losses sustained by the estate during the settlement of the estate, to the extent such losses are not compensated by insurance.[21]

The estate may also claim a "marital deduction" for the value of all property passing to the decedent's surviving spouse.[22] Only non-terminable interests passing to the surviving spouse qualify for this marital deduction. Interests that may terminate in favor of another person upon the lapse of time, the occurrence of an event or contingency, or the failure of an event or contingency to occur, generally do not qualify for the estate tax marital deduction.[23] Special exceptions to the terminable interest rule are made for certain transfers in trust of a lifetime income interest if the executor elects to include the value of the trust property in the surviving spouse's gross estate and for certain life estates coupled with a general power of appointment.[24] Certain life insurance settlement options and certain interests conditioned upon survivorship for a reasonable period not exceeding six months also serve as exceptions to the terminable interest rule.[25]

A deduction for certain charitable bequests and devises to qualified charitable organizations also reduce the value of the gross estate.[26] Although the rules are not identical, the estate tax charitable deduction functions similarly to its income tax counterpart with the purpose of encouraging charitable contributions.[27]

The gross estate is also reduced by the amount of any estate, inheritance, legacy, or succession taxes actually paid to any state or the District of Columbia in respect to property included in the gross estate.[28]

Computation of the Estate Tax

Under the unified estate and gift tax system, computation of a decedent's estate tax liability requires a "grossed-up," or a combination, of the decedent's lifetime taxable gifts and the decedent's taxable estate to which the tax rate schedule is then applied. Any available credits are subsequently taken to obtain the decedent's actual estate tax liability (the amount of tax to be paid by the estate).[29]

The estate rate schedule[30] is as follows:

Taxable Estate	Tentative Tax
not over $10,000	18% of such amount
$10,000-$20,000	$1,800 + 20% of excess over $10,000
$20,000-$40,000	$3,800 + 22% of excess over $20,000
$40,000-$60,000	$8,200 + 24% of excess over $40,000
$60,000-$80,000	$13,000 + 26% of excess over $60,000
$80,000-$100,000	$18,200 + 28% of excess over $80,000
$100,000-$150,000	$23,800 + 30% of excess over $100,000
$150,000-$250,000	$38,800 + 32% of excess over $150,000
$250,000-$500,000	$70,800 + 34% of excess over $250,000
$500,000 -$750,000	$155,800 + 37% of excess over $500,000
$750,000 -$1,000,000	$248,300 + 39% of excess over $750,000
Over $1,000,000	$345,800 + 40% of excess over $1,000,000

There are three major estate tax credits presently in effect: the unified transfer tax credit, the credit for foreign death taxes, and the credit for federal estate taxes paid by previous estates. Each credit is a dollar-for-dollar offset against an estate's federal estate tax liability.

The unified transfer tax credit is available against both lifetime gift tax liabilities and the estate tax liability. To the extent this credit is used to offset gift taxes, it is unavailable to offset estate taxes. The IRC refers to the credit as an "applicable exclusion amount," that is, the amount of taxable gifts or estate that the credit would cover.[31] The applicable exclusion amount in 2014 is $5,340,000.

Each estate may also use credits for foreign death taxes, including estate, inheritance, legacy, or succession taxes actually paid by the estate or any heir with respect to property included in the federal gross estate. This credit is limited to the amount of U.S. estate taxes paid on the same property. The credit is computed as the same proportionate share of the total U.S. estate taxes as the value of the foreign taxed property bears to the total of the U.S. taxable estate.[32]

The credit for previously taxed property (PTP credit) is provided to relieve some of the harshness that could otherwise result when an individual dies soon after inheriting property upon which a federal estate tax has already been imposed. The PTP credit is allowed for all or some portion of the federal estate taxes paid on property transferred to the decedent within the past ten years. The PTP credit is graduated according to the amount of time that has elapsed between the date the property was transferred to the decedent and the date of death. The maximum PTP credit is 100% of the previously paid taxes, when the decedent received the property within two years prior to the date of death. The minimum PTP credit is 20% of the previously paid taxes, when the decedent received the property during the ninth or tenth years preceding the date of death.[33]

THE FEDERAL GIFT TAX

The federal gift tax is a tax imposed on an annual basis on all gratuitous transfers of property made during life. The tax seeks to account for transfers of property that would otherwise reduce the estate and accordingly estate tax liability at death.[34] The donor's tax liability on the gift depends upon the value of the "taxable gift." The taxable gift is determined by reducing the gross value of the gift by the available deductions and exclusions. The gift tax liability created on the basis of the donor's taxable gifts may be reduced by the available unified transfer tax credit. This discussion will divide the federal gift tax into two components: the taxable gift and the computation of the gift tax.

The Taxable Gift

The donor calculates the gift tax liability by first determining the amount of the taxable gift. The amount of the taxable gift is the fair market value of the gift at the time it was made, less certain exclusions and deductions.[35] The major deductions and exclusions are the annual per donee exclusion, the gift tax marital deduction, and the gift tax charitable deduction.

Through the annual exclusion, every donor may exclude from his/her federal gift tax base the first $14,000 of cash or property given to each donee annually.[36] An unlimited exclusion is available for gifts of direct payments to the donee's educational institution for tuition expenses or to the donee's medical provider for health care expenses.[37] Under the present interest rule, the annual exclusion is unavailable, however, for gifts of future interests which vest in the donee only upon some future date. The present interest rule often requires complicated drafting techniques to obtain the annual exclusion for the value of a gift of a life insurance policy made in trust, or a gift to a minor, to be held in trust until the minor reaches a certain age.[38]

Married couples may double the annual exclusion through "gift-splitting," an arrangement in which one spouse consents to being treated as having made one-half of the gifts made by his or her spouse in that taxable year.[39] The election is made by a notation on the gift tax return, and results in each spouse receiving a $14,000 per donee exclusion for one-half of the value of the same gift. Therefore, married couples may annually exclude $28,000 per donee from their tax liability by gift-splitting.

Several deductions are also available for the donor to reduce his/her tax liability. A donor may deduct the value of certain interspousal gifts.[40] Like its estate tax counterpart, the gift tax marital deduction is not allowed for most gifts of terminable interests.[41] A donor may also deduct the value of certain charitable gifts. The value of the gift may be deducted only if the charity is of a type described in the applicable statutory provision, which describes most, but not all, of the charities for which deductible income tax contributions may be made.[42]

The division of property incident to a divorce or separation agreement may result in the interspousal transfer of property for consideration which is not adequate for gift tax purposes. Consequently, the IRC provides that interspousal transfers pursuant to a written agreement dividing the property of the spouses and occurring within one year before and two years after a decree of divorce will not be treated as taxable gifts. However, in order to meet this provision, the agreement must settle the marital rights of the spouses or provide for a reasonable allowance for the support of minor children.[43]

The renunciation of property given one by another person might be viewed as either the negation of the initial gift, resulting in no gift tax liability, or as a reciprocal gift, resulting in two gift tax liabilities. The gift will be ignored for gift tax purposes if a disclaimer is made in writing before the donee has accepted any benefits of the property and within nine months of the gift's date.[44]

Computation of the Gift Tax

The tax liability of a taxable gift is measured initially by the value of the transferred property.[45] The gift tax follows the same progressive rates as the estate tax.[46] The tax is then applied cumulatively to taxable gifts made over the donor's lifetime.

The actual computation of the gift tax for each calendar year is completed in three steps. First, the donor's taxable gifts for the calendar year and any preceding calendar periods are totaled and the tentative tax determined. Second, the tentative tax is again calculated using the total taxable gifts for preceding calendar periods. Third, the result from step two is subtracted from the result of step one, and the donor's unused unified tax credit is applied to the remaining amount.[47] The combination of the progressive tax rates and the cumulative computation of the gift tax generates the tax liability of larger gifts at progressively higher rates.

THE GENERATION-SKIPPING TRANSFER TAX

The Tax Reform Act of 1986 repealed the original generation-skipping transfer (GST) tax, enacted in 1976, because of its complexity and replaced it with a simplified flat-rate tax.[48] The purpose of the resulting GST tax is the same as its predecessor, to close a loophole in the estate and gift tax system where property could be transferred to successive generations without paying multiple estate or gift taxes. The traditional generation-skipping transfers were trusts established by a parent for the lifetime benefit of the children with the remainder passing to the grandchildren. If properly drafted, an estate or gift tax would not be imposed when the trust corpus passed from the settlor's children to the settlor's grandchildren because the estate tax is not imposed on interests that terminate at death. This discussion will divide the generation-skipping transfer tax into two components: generation-skipping transfers and the computation of the tax.

Generation-Skipping Transfers

The GST tax is a flat-rate tax. The rate is set at the highest estate tax rate, currently 40%.[49] This tax rate is applied to three different transfer events: a direct skip, a taxable termination, or a taxable distribution.

A direct skip is a transfer to a skip person. A skip person is a person assigned to a generation two or more generations below the transferor's.[50] A transfer to a trust is a direct skip if all the interests in the trust are held by skip persons.[51] A taxable termination is a termination by death, lapse of time, release of power, or otherwise of an interest in property held in trust. A taxable termination does not occur if immediately after the termination a non-skip person has an interest in the property or if after the termination, the trust makes a distribution to a skip person.[52] A taxable distribution is a distribution from a trust, other than a taxable termination or direct skip, to a skip person.[53]

An important step in determining the GST tax is to assign all persons involved to a specific generation level, as outlined in the IRC.[54] Persons related to the transferor or spouse are assigned along family lines. For example, the transferor, spouse, and brothers and sisters are in one generation, their children in the next, and grandchildren in the next. Lineal descendants of a grandparent of the transferor or spouse are assigned to generations on the same basis. Anyone ever married to a lineal descendant of the transferor's grandparent or the spouse's grandparent are assigned to the level of their spouse who was a lineal descendant. Non-relatives of the transferor are assigned generations measured from the birth of the transferor. Persons not more than 121/2 years younger are treated as members of the same generation as the transferor. Each 25-year period thereafter is treated as a new generation. A grandchild of the transferor or spouse is moved up one generation if his parents are deceased at the time of the transfer.[55]

Computation of the Generation-Skipping Transfer Tax

The first step in calculating the GST tax is to determine the taxable amount. For direct skips, the taxable amount is the value of the property received by the transferee.[56] The GST tax on direct skips is tax-exclusive, meaning that the amount of tax paid is proportional to the pretax value of the transferred property. Contrastingly, the taxable amount for taxable terminations and distributions is tax-inclusive. The taxable amount for these property transfers is determined by including the tax value with the value of the property before applying the tax rate.

The second step in calculating the GST tax is to apply the applicable rate. The applicable rate is the maximum Federal estate tax rate (40% for 2014) and the inclusion ratio of the transfer.[57] The inclusion ratio is figured by subtracting from one ("1") the following fraction: the portion of the GST exemption allocated to the transfer as the numerator and the value of the property transferred as the denominator.[58] To compute the generation-skipping tax, the value of the transfer is multiplied by the tax rate (40%) and by the inclusion ratio.[59]

The IRC provides several exemptions and exclusions for the GST tax.[60] Unlike the estate and gift taxes, the GST tax does not use the unified credit. Instead, a $5,340,000 GST exemption is allowed to each individual for generation-skipping transfers during life or at death.[61] The exemption is doubled for married individuals who elect to treat the transfers as made one-half by each spouse.[62] An indirect skip property transfer automatically triggers the GST exemption.[63] An indirect skip occurs when the generation one level below the decedent (e.g., children) receives some beneficial interest in the property before the property passes to the generation two or more levels below (e.g., grandchildren).

The exclusions for tuition and medical expense payments from the gift tax[64] also apply to the generation-skipping tax.[65] Additionally, the $14,000 per donee annual exclusion from the gift tax is recognized against taxation of direct skips only (i.e., where the property passes directly to the generation two or more levels below the decedent).[66]

The liability for the tax is determined by the type of transfer. In the case of a taxable distribution, the tax is paid by the transferee. The tax on taxable terminations or direct skips from a trust is paid by the trustee. Direct skips, other than those from a trust, are taxed to the transferor.[67]

End Notes

[1] P.L. 107-16, 107th Cong., 1st Sess. (2001).
[2] P.L. 111-312, 111th Cong., 2nd Sess. (2010).
[3] P.L. 112-240, 112th Cong., 2nd Sess. (2012).
[4] 26 U.S.C. §2031(a).
[5] 26 U.S.C. §2042.
[6] Treas. Regs. (26 C.F.R.) §20.2042-1(c)(2).
[7] 26 U.S.C. §2039(a). Annuities are valued according to the actuarial life expectancy of the annuitant, the frequency of the payments, and the size of the payments. Treas. Regs. (26 C.F.R.) §20.2039-1.
[8] 26 U.S.C. §2040(a). The right of survivorship is the power of the successor of a deceased individual to acquire that individual's property upon his/her death.
[9] 26 U.S.C. §2040(b).
[10] Because the gross estate may include property given away during the decedent's life, the gross estate for tax purposes is not the equivalent of the probate estate. See 26 U.S.C. §§2035, 2037.
[11] 26 U.S.C. §2036. A life interest in property is an interest which ceases upon the interest-holder's death. The retention of an estate, the duration of which is not ascertainable except with reference to the lifetime of the donor, is treated as a retained life interest. The retention of the right to vote shares of stock of certain closely-held corporations is also a retained life interest. 26 U.S.C. §2036(b); see also, United States v. Byrum, 408 U.S. 125 (1972).
[12] 26 U.S.C. §2038. These transfers are also known as "revocable transfers" because the retained power allowed the deceased donor to revoke the transfer and return to himself or herself the enjoyment of the transferred property.
[13] 26 U.S.C. §2037.
[14] 26 U.S.C. §2041.
[15] 26 U.S.C. §2041. Certain other powers are statutorily classified as limited or non-special powers of appointment, including the right to invade the corpus (principal) subject only to an ascertainable standard relating to health, education, support or maintenance; or the non-cumulative right to withdraw up to the greater of $5,000 or 5% of corpus annually.
[16] 26 U.S.C. §2032(a). The alternate valuation date is useful when the value of the property contained in the gross estate has decreased following the death of the decedent, such as might be the case when the estate holds a substantial quantity of stock in a corporation in which the decedent was a dominant figure.
[17] Treas. Regs. (26 C.F.R.) §20.2031-1(b).
[18] Id.
[19] See Treas. Regs. (26 C.F.R.) §§20.2031-1 – 20.2031-10.
[20] 26 U.S.C. §2053.
[21] 26 U.S.C. §2054.
[22] 26 U.S.C. §2056. Generally, the unlimited marital deduction is not allowed for transfers to a surviving spouse who is not a citizen of the United States and does not become a citizen before the estate tax return is filed unless the transfer utilizes a qualified domestic trust. See 26 U.S.C. §2056(d). A qualified domestic trust is defined in 26 U.S.C. §2056A to be a trust that has at least one trustee who is a United States citizen and such citizen trustee has veto power over distributions from the trust.
[23] 26 U.S.C. §2056(b). Known as the "terminable interest rule."
[24] Id.

[25] Id.
[26] 26 U.S.C. §2055.
[27] Compare 26 U.S.C. §§2055(a) and 170(c).
[28] 26 U.S.C. §2058.
[29] 26 U.S.C. §2001(b).
[30] 26 U.S.C. §2001(c). The taxable estate is the gross estate less any relevant deductions. The tax rate is then applied to the taxable estate resulting in the tentative tax. Any available credits are then taken from the tentative tax to arrive at the estate's actual tax liability.
[31] 26 U.S.C. §2010.
[32] 26 U.S.C. §2014.
[33] 26 U.S.C. §2013.
[34] The word "gift" is not defined in the IRC, but the statute does state that the amount of a gift is ascertained when "property is transferred for less than an adequate and full consideration in money or money's worth." 26 U.S.C. §2512(b). Generally, IRS regulations state that a gift is made, for gift tax purposes, when there is a transfer for inadequate consideration and the transaction does not take place in a business context. Treas. Regs. (26 C.F.R.) §25.2511. This should be distinguished from the definition of a "gift" for income tax purposes, which requires that the transfer be made from "detached and disinterested generosity." Comm'r v. Duberstein, 363 U.S. 278 (1960). A transfer may, therefore, be a gift for gift tax purposes, because there was no legally sufficient consideration, but not constitute a gift for income tax purposes, because it was not motivated by detached and disinterested generosity.
[35] 26 U.S.C. §2512. Special valuation rules for valuation freezing transactions are set forth in 26 U.S.C. §2701 through 2704.
[36] 26 U.S.C. §2503. This figure is indexed for inflation.
[37] 26 U.S.C. §2503(e).
[38] But see 26 U.S.C. §2503(c), for a special rule granting the annual exclusion for gifts to certain trusts created for the benefit of minors that permit the income to be expended for the benefit of the minor until the minor attains age 21 and require the minor to be given outright ownership of the trust assets at that age or, if the minor should die prior to attaining age 21, to designate by will or otherwise the disposition of the property.
[39] 26 U.S.C. §2513. Gift-splitting also permits use of both spouses' unified transfer tax credits to eliminate present tax on lifetime taxable gifts.
[40] 26 U.S.C. §2523(a).
[41] 26 U.S.C. §2523(b), (f).
[42] Compare 26 U.S.C. §2522 and §170(c).
[43] 26 U.S.C. §2516.
[44] 26 U.S.C. §2518.
[45] 26 U.S.C. §2501.
[46] 26 U.S.C. §2001(c).
[47] 26 U.S.C. §§2502, 2001(c), 2505. P.L. 111-312 restored the total unification of the unified credit so that the full applicable exclusion amount is available to offset gifts. The 40% top rate must be used for computing the amount of credit used when grossing up any previously made gifts where a higher rate was used.
[48] Staff of the Joint Committee on Taxation, 100th Cong., 1st Sess., General Explanation of the Tax Reform Act of 1986, 1263 (1987). P.L. 11-312 brought back the generation-skipping transfer tax after a hiatus for 2010.
[49] 26 U.S.C. §2641(a).
[50] 26 U.S.C. §2613.

[51] 26 U.S.C. §2612.
[52] 26 U.S.C. §2612.
[53] 26 U.S.C. §2612.
[54] 26 U.S.C. §2651.
[55] 26 U.S.C. §2651.
[56] 26 U.S.C. §2623.
[57] 26 U.S.C. §2641.
[58] 26 U.S.C. §2642.
[59] 26 U.S.C. §2641.
[60] See e.g., P.L. 99-514, §1433(b)(3) provided that for transfers made prior to January 1, 1990, each grantor could exempt $2,000,000 in direct skips per grandchild ($4,000,000 for married individuals who elect to treat the transfers as made one-half by each spouse).
[61] 26 U.S.C. §2631(a). The GST exemption is equal to the estate tax unified credit amount, with both indexed for inflation. The GST exemption may be allocated by the transferor or the executor to any generation-skipping transfer. The allocation is irrevocable once made. Unless a contrary election is made, all or any portion of the exclusion not previously allocated is deemed allocated to a lifetime direct skip to the extent necessary to make the inclusion ratio for the transfer zero. 26 U.S.C. §2632.
[62] 26 U.S.C. §2652(a).
[63] 26 U.S.C. §2632(c).
[64] 26 U.S.C. §2503(e).
[65] 26 U.S.C. §2611(b).
[66] 26 U.S.C. §2642(c).
[67] 26 U.S.C. §2603.

In: Federal Taxation of Wealth Transfers
Editor: Jerry Washington
ISBN: 978-1-63482-991-5

Chapter 2

HISTORY, PRESENT LAW, AND ANALYSIS OF THE FEDERAL WEALTH TRANSFER TAX SYSTEM[*]

Joint Committee on Taxation

I. OVERVIEW

The Subcommittee on Select Revenue Measures of the House Committee on Ways and Means has scheduled a public hearing for March 18, 2015, on the burden of the estate tax on family businesses and farms.

This document[1] provides a history, description, and analysis of the Federal estate, gift, and generation-skipping transfer taxes (also referred to herein as the "wealth transfer taxes"), as well as a description of selected reform proposals.

The overview presents data about wealth transfer taxes, a brief discussion of possible economic effects of the taxes, and a short summary of present-law rules.

---

[*] This is an edited, reformatted and augmented version of a Committee report, JCX-52-15, issued March 16, 2015.

Data About the Federal Estate and Gift Tax

Revenues generated by the estate and gift tax are a small portion of overall Federal tax revenues. In fiscal year 2014, the IRS collected $19.3 billion in net estate and gift tax revenues. This amount represented 0.6 percent of total net Federal tax collections in fiscal year 2014. By comparison, the highest post-World War II share of total Federal revenues represented by the estate and gift tax was 2.6 percent in fiscal year 1972.[2]

Relatively few taxpayers are directly affected by the Federal estate and gift tax. In 2013, the most recent year for which final numbers are available, there were 2.6 million deaths in the United States, and 4,700 estate tax returns reporting some tax liability were filed. Thus, taxable estate tax returns represented approximately one-fifth of one percent of deaths in 2013. By comparison, in the mid-1970s taxable estate tax returns exceeded six percent of all deaths.

Economic Ramifications of Estate Taxation

Although the Federal estate and gift tax accounts for a small share of total Federal revenues and directly affects a small percentage of taxpayers, it may have broad economic effects. First, the estate tax might affect aggregate capital formation, but there is not consensus among economists on this issue. Some economists believe that individuals' attitudes toward leaving bequests have a significant effect on overall capital accumulation. The existence of an estate tax may influence these attitudes.

Second, the estate tax may affect individuals' saving behavior. Because the estate tax increases the after-tax cost of leaving a bequest, the existence of the tax may discourage some individuals from saving for a bequest. On the other hand, individuals who want to give a bequest of a certain amount may increase their savings to account for the potential estate tax burden. There has been limited empirical analysis to determine the effect, if any, of the estate tax on individual saving.

Third, the estate tax may have an impact on the amount of investment in small businesses. An estate tax might create cash flow difficulties for small businesses and thereby may cause small business owners to borrow money or to sell or otherwise liquidate businesses to pay estate tax liability. If small businesses are sold, there may be a shift toward less overall investment in small business. If small business owners borrow funds to pay the estate tax, they may reduce their investment in the businesses, and this reduced investment could have deleterious effects on the larger economy. Some observers argue, however, that the present estate tax imposes a limited burden on small business owners because the exemption level has risen to $5.43 million for estates of individuals dying in 2015 and because special rules allow installment payment of tax liability for estates consisting largely of closely-held business assets.

Another way in which the estate tax may affect the economy is through planning strategies to avoid the tax. To the extent that resources are shifted towards tax avoidance activities and away from more productive endeavors, the overall economy may be smaller as a result.

Current Estate and Gift Tax Rules

In general, a gift tax is imposed on certain lifetime transfers and an estate tax is imposed on certain transfers at death. A generation-skipping transfer tax generally is imposed on certain transfers, made either directly or in trust or using a similar arrangement, to a "skip person" (*i.e.*, a beneficiary in a generation more than one generation younger than that of the transferor).

A unified credit is available with respect to taxable transfers by gift and at death.[3] The unified credit offsets tax computed at the lowest estate and gift tax rates on a specified amount of transfers, referred to as the applicable exclusion amount, or exemption amount. The exemption amount was set at $5 million for 2010 and 2011 and is indexed for inflation for years after 2011. For 2015, the inflation-indexed estate and gift tax exemption amount is $5.43 million.[4] An election is available under which any exemption that remains unused as of a decedent's death generally is available for use by a surviving spouse (sometimes referred to as exemption portability). The top estate and gift tax rate is 40 percent.

Donors of lifetime gifts are provided an inflation-indexed annual exclusion of $14,000 per donee in 2015 for gifts of present interests in property during the taxable year. In addition, gifts and bequests to a spouse or to charity generally are not subject to gift tax or estate tax. A Federal estate tax deduction is allowed for certain death taxes paid to any foreign country, State or the District of Columbia.

Property acquired from a donor of a lifetime gift generally takes a carryover basis. "Carryover basis" means that the basis in the hands of the donee is the same as it was in the hands of the donor. Property acquired from a decedent's estate generally takes a stepped-up basis. "Stepped-up basis" means that the basis of property acquired from a decedent's estate generally is the fair market value on the date of the decedent's death (or, if the alternate valuation date is elected, the earlier of six months after the decedent's death or the date the property is sold or distributed by the estate).

Lawmakers and the Administration have offered numerous proposals to modify the present-law rules. Part V describes several recent proposals to: (1) repeal the estate and generation-skipping transfer taxes; (2) expand the taxation of wealth transfers by decreasing exemption amounts and increasing tax rates; (3) expand the transfer tax base; and (4) impose a new tax on the transfer of built-in gains at the time of a gift or upon a decedent's death.

II. History of the U.S. Wealth Transfer Tax System

A. In General

Wealth transfer were first introduced into the U.S. Federal tax system in 1797. The present-law Federal wealth transfer tax system consists of three related components: a gift tax, an estate tax, and a generation-skipping transfer tax.

Over much of the past two decades, the estate and gift tax laws have remained in flux, creating uncertainty for taxpayers and their advisors. The Economic Growth and Tax Relief Reconciliation Act of 2001 ("EGTRRA")[5] gradually phased out the Federal estate and generation-skipping taxes from 2002 through 2009, principally through nearly annual increases in exemption amounts and reductions in applicable tax rates. EGTRRA then provided for a single-year repeal of the estate tax, only for decedents dying in 2010.

EGTRRA was scheduled to sunset at the end of 2010, with the estate and gift tax laws to revert to the structure that would have been in effect if EGTRRA had never been enacted (generally, a lower exemption amount and higher tax rates). Congress intervened in December 2010[6] and again in January 2013,[7] ultimately establishing what is now a permanent estate and gift tax regime with a higher exemption amount ($5.43 million for 2015) that is indexed for inflation and a top rate of 40 percent.

B. Federal Taxes on Transfers at Death before World War I

While States extensively used transfer taxes at death for various purposes, Federal taxes on transfers at death in the United States, for most of its history, were imposed primarily to finance wars or the threat of war. The first Federal tax on such transfers was imposed from 1797 until 1802 as a stamp tax on inventories of deceased persons, receipts of legacies, shares of personal estate, probates of wills, and letters of administration to pay for the development of strong naval forces felt necessary because of strained trade relations with France.[8] After repeal of the stamp tax,[9] there were no death-related taxes imposed by the Federal government until the Civil War, when the Federal government imposed an inheritance tax[10] between 1862 and 1870.[11]

To finance the Spanish-American War, the Federal government imposed its first estate tax in 1898, [12] which remained in effect until its repeal in 1902.[13]

While prior death-related taxes were imposed primarily to finance warfare, in 1906 President Theodore Roosevelt proposed a progressive tax on all lifetime gifts and death-time bequests specifically for the purpose of limiting the amount that one individual could transfer to another and thereby to break up large concentrations of wealth. No legislation immediately resulted from the proposal.[14]

C. Estate Taxes from World War I Through World War II

Estate Taxes to finance World War I

The commencement of World War I caused revenues from tariffs to fall. The Federal government in 1916[15] enacted a progressive estate tax on all property owned by the decedent at his or her death, certain lifetime transfers which were for inadequate consideration,[16] transfers not intended to take effect until death,[17] and transfers made in contemplation of death.

The 1916 estate tax, which in many respects was similar to the present-day estate tax, provided an exemption (in the form of a deduction) of $50,000 with rates from one percent on the first $50,000 of transferred assets to 10 percent on transferred assets in excess of $5 million. The next year, the revenue needs from the war resulted in increases in estate tax rates, with a top rate of 25 percent on transferred assets in excess of $10 million.[18]

Estate and Gift Taxes between World Wars I and II

Following the end of World War I, Congress debated whether an estate tax remained necessary. In the Revenue Act of 1918, the estate tax was retained, but estate tax rates on transfers under $1 million were reduced. At the same time, the tax was extended to life insurance proceeds in excess of $40,000 that were receivable by the estate or its executor and to property subject to a general power of appointment.[19]

In 1924, the estate tax was changed by: (1) increasing the maximum rate to 40 percent; (2) broadening property subject to the tax to include jointly-owned property and property subject to a power retained by the decedent to alter, amend, or revoke the beneficial enjoyment of the property;[20] and (3) allowing a credit for State death-related taxes of up to 25 percent of the Federal tax. In addition, the first gift tax was imposed, using the estate tax rate schedule.

In response to opposition to the estate and gift taxes, in 1926, the gift tax was repealed and estate tax rates were reduced to a maximum rate of 20 percent on transfers over $10 million. The exemption was increased from $50,000 to $100,000, and the credit for State death taxes was increased to 80 percent of the Federal tax.

With the Great Depression, revenues from other sources were declining, and the need for new revenues for government projects increased. As a result, in 1932 estate tax rates were increased, with a top rate of 45 percent on transfers over $10 million.[21] The tax was made applicable to lifetime transfers in which the transferor retained a life estate or the power to control who benefits from the property or income from such property.[22] The exemption was reduced to $50,000, and the Federal gift tax was reimposed (at 75 percent of the estate tax rates) for cumulative lifetime gifts in excess of $5,000 per year.

Estate and gift tax rates were further increased in 1934 with the highest marginal rates of 60 percent and 45 percent, respectively, applying to transfers in excess of $10 million. Estate and gift tax rates were increased again in 1935 with the highest marginal rates of 70 percent and 52.5 percent, respectively, applying to transfers in excess of $50 million.[23] The exemption for both the estate and gift tax was modified in 1935 to $40,000 each.[24]

In 1940, a 10-percent surcharge was imposed on both income and estate and gift taxes, in light of the need for additional revenue necessitated by the military build-up just prior to World War II.[25] Estate and gift tax rates were increased in 1941, with a top estate tax rate of 77 percent on transfers in excess of $50 million.[26]

Estate and Gift Taxes during World War II

In 1942, Congress again altered estate and gift taxes by: (1) setting the exemption from the estate tax at $60,000, setting the lifetime exemption from gift tax at $30,000,[27] and providing an annual gift tax exclusion of $3,000; and (2) attempting to equate property in community property States with property owned in non-community property States by providing that in both community property States and non-community property States, each spouse would be taxed on the portion of jointly-owned or community property that each spouse contributed to that property's acquisition cost.[28]

D. Estate and Gift Taxes after World War II

Post-World War II through 1975

The 1942 solution to the community property problem was viewed as complex. Congress provided a different solution in 1948 for equating community property States and non-community property States by providing the decedent or donor spouse a marital deduction for 50 percent of the property transferred to the other spouse, and, thus, effectively allowing both spouses to be taxed on one-half of the property's value.[29]

In 1954, the estate tax treatment of life insurance was changed. Under a new rule, life insurance was subject to estate tax if the proceeds were paid to the decedent's estate or executor or if the decedent retained "incidents of ownership" in the life insurance policy.[30]

The Small Business Tax Revision Act of 1958[31] provided for payment of Federal estate tax on certain closely-held businesses in installments over a 10-year period.[32]

Legislation from 1976 through 1980

In the Tax Reform Act of 1976 ("the 1976 Act"),[33] Congress substantially revised estate and gift taxes. The 1976 Act unified the estate and gift taxes, such that a single graduated rate schedule with a maximum rate of 70 percent applied to transfers during life and at death.[34] As under present law, lifetime gifts were cumulative, with successive gifts potentially subject to higher rates, and transfers at death stacked on top of cumulative lifetime gifts for purposes of determining the applicable marginal rate on such transfers. In addition, the estate and gift tax exclusions were combined into a single "unified credit," which at the time effectively exempted $175,625 of transfers from tax when fully phased in. The 1976 Act also changed the income tax rules applicable to the disposition of inherited assets from a rule that only taxed post-death appreciation (*i.e.*, the basis in the hands of the heir was "stepped up" to its value on the date of the decedent's death) to one that provided that the heir's basis generally would be the same as it was in the hands of the decedent (*i.e.*, the decedent's basis in the property would "carry over" to be the basis to the heir). In addition, the 1976 Act provided a 100-percent marital deduction for the first $250,000 of property transferred to a surviving spouse.

Another significant change in 1976 was the imposition of a new transfer tax on generation-skipping transfers generally equal to the additional estate or gift tax that the decedent's children would have paid if the property had passed directly to the children instead of skipping that generation and passing to, for example, a donor's or decedent's grandchildren.

The 1976 Act also included preferential rules for valuing family farms and small business held in estates. Specifically, the law provided that a farm or other real property used in a closely- held business could be valued at its current-use value rather than its highest and best use value, so long as the heirs continue to use the property for 15 years after the decedent's death; and liberalized the provision that permits installment payments of estate tax on closely-held businesses by providing that only interest need be paid for the first four years after death and by lengthening the period of installment by an additional four years.[35]

In 1980, the estate tax carryover basis rules were retroactively repealed and replaced with the step-up basis rules.[36]

Legislation from 1981 through 1985

The Economic Recovery Tax Act of 1981 (the "1981 Act")[37] made a number of changes to the estate and gift tax rules, many of which either had the effect of reducing the number of taxable estates or reduced or eliminated taxes on transfers between spouses. For example, the 1981 Act increased the unified credit such that, when fully phased in in 1987, it effectively exempted the first $600,000 of transfers from the unified estate and gift tax, and reduced the top unified estate and gift tax rate from 70 percent to 50 percent over a four-year period (1982 through 1985). The 1981 Act provided an unlimited deduction for transfers to spouses and permitted such a deduction even when the donee spouse could not control the disposition of the property after that spouse's death, so long as the spouse had an income interest in the property and the property was subject to that spouse's estate and gift tax (referred to as "qualified terminable interest property"). Additionally, the 1981 Act) modified the special-use valuation rules by shortening to 10 years the period that heirs who inherit farms or other real property used in a closely held business were required to so use the property, and increased the maximum reduction in value of such property from $500,000 to $750,000; and further liberalized and simplified the rules that permit the installment payment of estate tax on closely-held businesses.[38]

The Deficit Reduction Act of 1984 made a number of additional modifications to the estate and gift tax rules.[39]

Legislation from 1986 through 1997

The Tax Reform Act of 1986[40] substantially revised the tax on generation-skipping transfers by applying a single rate of tax equal to the highest estate tax rate (*i.e.*, 55 percent) to all generation-skipping transfers in excess of $1 million and by broadening the definition of a generation-skipping transfer to include direct transfers from a grandparent to a grandchild (*i.e.*, direct skips).

The Omnibus Budget Reconciliation Act of 1987[41] modified the estate and gift tax by: (1) providing special rules under which so-called "estate freeze transactions" result in the inclusion in the decedent's gross estate of the total value of property transferred; (2) providing a higher estate or gift tax rate on transfers in excess of $10 million to phase out the benefit of the graduated rates under 55 percent and the benefit of the unified credit; and (3) again delaying the scheduled reduction in the estate and gift tax rates from 55 percent to 50 percent for five years.

The Omnibus Budget Reconciliation Act of 1990[42] replaced the special rules for estate freeze transactions with a new set of rules that effectively subject to gift tax the full value of interests in property, unless retained interests in that property take certain specified forms.[43]

The maximum estate, gift, and generation-skipping transfer tax rate dropped to 50 percent after December 31, 1992, but the Omnibus Budget Reconciliation Act of 1993[44] restored the 55- percent top rate retroactively to January 1, 1993, and made that top rate permanent. The Taxpayer Relief Act of 1997[45] provided for gradual increases in the unified credit effective exemption amount from $625,000 in 1998 to $1 million in 2006 and thereafter. Under a conforming amendment to the five-percent surtax, the benefit of the graduated rates, but not the benefit of the unified credit, was phased out. A new exclusion for qualified conservation easements and a new deduction for interests in qualified family-owned businesses, in addition to other changes, also were enacted in 1997.

The Economic Growth and Tax Relief Reconciliation Act of 2001 ("EGTRRA")[46]

EGTRRA signaled an attempt to reduce or eliminate the Federal estate and generation-skipping taxes by phasing out and ultimately repealing those taxes. EGTRRA phased out the estate and generation-skipping taxes through 2009 by gradually increasing the lifetime estate tax exemption to $3.5 million and reducing the top estate tax rate to 45 percent. In addition, the credit for State death taxes paid was reduced and, for estates of decedents dying after 2004, replaced by a deduction for such taxes. In 2010, the estate and generation-skipping taxes were to be repealed, though only for one year, after which the estate tax exemption would drop to $1 million with a top tax rate of 55 percent. The basis in assets transferred from a decedent who died in 2010 would no longer be stepped up; instead, a modified carryover basis regime was to take effect.

E. Recent Legislation

Reinstatement of the Estate Tax for 2010 and Temporary Extension of the Modified Estate and Gift Tax Laws through 2012

Although EGTRRA had provided for temporary repeal of the estate and generation-skipping transfer taxes for deaths and transfers occurring in 2010, the Tax Relief, Unemployment Insurance Reauthorization, and Job Creation Act of 2010 (the "2010 Act"), enacted December 17, 2010, retroactively reinstated the estate and generation-skipping transfer taxes effective January 1, 2010, and extended the new rules through 2012. The estate tax exemption was increased to $5 million for 2010 and 2011 (and was indexed for inflation for years after 2011), and the top estate and gift tax rate was set at 35 percent. Beginning in 2011, the gift tax was reunified with the estate tax - *i.e.*, the gift tax exemption was raised to equal the estate tax exemption. The 2010 Act also repealed the EGTRRA modified carryover basis rules that were scheduled to be in effect for assets acquired from a decedent who died in 2010, such that the basis generally was stepped up to fair market value. Under the 2010 Act, any unused exemption of a decedent who died after 2010 generally was available for use by a surviving spouse (exemption portability).

To mitigate the effect of retroactively reinstating the estate tax, in the case of a decedent who died during 2010, the 2010 Act allowed the executor to elect to apply the Internal Revenue Code as if the reinstated estate tax and basis step-up rules described in the preceding paragraph had not been enacted.

In other words, the executor could elect to have the law as originally enacted under EGTRRA apply for 2010 decedents, *i.e.*, repeal of the estate tax, accompanied by application of the less generous modified carryover basis rules for assets acquired from a decedent.

Permanent Extension of the Estate and Gift Tax Laws with an Inflation-Indexed Exemption Amount

The American Taxpayer Relief Act of 2012 made permanent the estate and gift tax laws that were in effect in 2012, but increased the top estate and gift tax rate to 40 percent. Thus, for all years after 2012, the estate and gift taxes are unified with an exemption amount that is indexed for inflation (from $5 million in 2011). For 2013, 2014, and 2015, the inflation-indexed exemption amounts are $5.25 million, $5.34 million, and $5.43 million, respectively.

The present-law estate and gift tax regime is discussed in greater detail in Part III, below.

F. Summary

Table 1 provides a summary of the annual gift tax exclusion, the exemption value of the unified credit, the threshold level of the highest statutory estate tax rate, and the highest statutory estate tax rate for selected years, 1977 through 2015.

Table 1. Estate and Gift Tax Rates and Exemption Amounts, 1977-2015

Year	Annual gift exclusion per donee single/joint	Exemption value of unified credit	Threshold of highest statutory tax rate[1]	Highest statutory tax rate (percent)
1977	$3,000/$6,000	$120,667	$5 million	70
1982	$10,000/$20,000	$225,000	$4 million	65
1983	$10,000/$20,000	$275,000	$3.5 million	60
1984	$10,000/$20,000	$325,000	$3 million	55
1985	$10,000/$20,000	$400,000	$3 million	55
1986	$10,000/$20,000	$500,000	$3 million	55
1987	$10,000/$20,000	$600,000	$3 million	55 [2]
1998	$10,000/$20,000	$625,000	$3 million	55 [2]
1999	$10,000/$20,000	$650,000	$3 million	55 [2]

Table 1. (Continued)

Year	Annual gift exclusion per donee single/joint	Exemption value of unified credit	Threshold of highest statutory tax rate[1]	Highest statutory tax rate (percent)
2000	$10,000/$20,000	$675,000	$3 million	55 [2]
2002	$11,000/$22,000	$1 million	$2.5 million	50
2003	$11,000/$22,000	$1 million	$2 million	49
2004	$11,000/$22,000	$1.5 million	$2 million	48
2005	$11,000/$22,000	$1.5 million	$2 million	47
2006	$12,000/$24,000	$2 million	$2 million[1]	46
2007	$12,000/$24,000	$2 million	$1.5 million[1]	45
2009	$13,000/$26,000	$3.5 million	$1.5 million[1]	45
2010	$13,000/$26,000	$5 million	$500,000 [1]	35[3]
2012	$13,000/$26,000	$5.12 million	$500,000 [1]	35
2013	$14,000/$28,000	$5.25 million	$1 million [1]	40
2014	$14,000/$28,000	$5.34 million	$1 million [1]	40
2015	$14,000/$28,000	$5.43 million	$1 million[1]	40

[1] Because the exemption amount in later years equals or exceeds the threshold for the highest tax rate, transfers that equal or are in excess of the exemption amount generally are subject to a flat tax at the highest marginal rate.

[2] From 1987 through 1997, the benefits of the graduated rate structure and unified credit were phased out at a 5-percent rate for estates between $10,000,000 and $21,040,000, creating an effective marginal tax rate of 60 percent for affected estates (with a $600,000 unified credit). The Taxpayer Relief Act of 1997 provided for gradual increases in the unified credit from $625,000 in 1998 to $1 million in 2006 and thereafter. A conforming amendment made to the 5-percent surtax continued to phase out the benefit of the graduated rates, but the benefit of the unified credit was no longer phased out.

[3] As described in section II.E, above, for decedents dying in 2010, executors were permitted to elect not to have the estate subject to estate tax. Heirs who acquire assets from an electing decedent's estate, however, took a modified carryover basis determined under then-section 1022 of the Code, instead of a stepped-up basis determined under section 1014 of the Code.

III. Description of Present Law

A. In General

A gift tax is imposed on certain lifetime transfers, and an estate tax is imposed on certain transfers at death. A generation-skipping transfer tax generally is imposed on transfers, either directly or in trust or similar arrangement, to a "skip person" (*i.e.*, a beneficiary in a generation more than one generation younger than that of the transferor). Transfers subject to the generation-skipping transfer tax include direct skips, taxable terminations, and taxable distributions.

Income tax rules determine the recipient's tax basis in property acquired from a decedent or by gift. Gifts and bequests generally are excluded from the recipient's gross income.[47]

B. Common Features of the Estate, Gift and Generation-Skipping Transfer Taxes

Unified Credit (Exemption) and Tax Rates

Unified Credit

A unified credit is available with respect to taxable transfers by gift and at death.[48] The unified credit offsets tax computed at the lowest estate and gift tax rates on a specified amount of transfers, referred to as the applicable exclusion amount, or exemption amount. The exemption amount was set at $5 million for 2011 and is indexed for inflation for later years.[49] For 2015, the inflation-indexed exemption amount is $5.43 million.[50] Exemption used during life to offset taxable gifts reduces the amount of exemption that remains at death to offset the value of a decedent's estate. An election is available under which exemption that is not used by a decedent may be used by the decedent's surviving spouse (exemption portability).

Common Tax Rate Table

A common tax-rate table with a top marginal tax rate of 40 percent is used to compute gift tax and estate tax. The 40-percent rate applies to transfers in excess of $1 million (to the extent not exempt). Because the exemption amount currently shields the first $5.43 million in gifts and bequests from tax, transfers in excess of the exemption amount generally are subject to tax at the highest marginal 40-percent rate.

Generation-Skipping Transfer Tax Exemption and Rate

The generation-skipping transfer tax is a separate tax that can apply in addition to either the gift tax or the estate tax. The tax rate and exemption amount for generation-skipping transfer tax purposes, however, are set by reference to the estate tax rules. Generation-skipping transfer tax is imposed using a flat rate equal to the highest estate tax rate (40 percent). Tax is imposed on cumulative generation-skipping transfers in excess of the generation-skipping transfer tax exemption amount in effect for the year of the transfer. The generation-skipping transfer tax exemption for a given year is equal to the estate tax exemption amount in effect for that year (currently $5.43 million).

Transfers between Spouses

In General

A 100-percent marital deduction generally is permitted for the value of property transferred between spouses.[51] In addition, transfers of "qualified terminable interest property" also are eligible for the marital deduction. Qualified terminable interest property is property: (1) that passes from the decedent, (2) in which the surviving spouse has a "qualifying income interest for life," and (3) to which an election under these rules applies. A qualifying income interest for life exists if: (1) the surviving spouse is entitled to all the income from the property (payable annually or at more frequent intervals) or has the right to use the property during the spouse's life, and (2) no person has the power to appoint any part of the property to any person other than the surviving spouse.

Transfers to Surviving Spouses Who Are Not U.S. Citizens

A marital deduction generally is denied for property passing to a surviving spouse who is not a citizen of the United States. A marital deduction is permitted, however, for property passing to a qualified domestic trust of which the noncitizen surviving spouse is a beneficiary. A qualified domestic trust is a trust that has as its trustee at least one U.S. citizen or U.S. corporation. No corpus may be distributed from a qualified domestic trust unless the U.S. trustee has the right to withhold any estate tax imposed on the distribution.

Tax is imposed on (1) any distribution from a qualified domestic trust before the date of the death of the noncitizen surviving spouse and (2) the value of the property remaining in a qualified domestic trust on the date of death of the noncitizen surviving spouse. The tax is computed as an additional estate tax on the estate of the first spouse to die.

Transfers to Charity

Contributions to charitable and certain other organizations may be deducted from the value of a gift or from the value of the assets in an estate for Federal gift or estate tax purposes.[52]

The effect of the deduction generally is to remove the full fair market value of assets transferred to charity from the gift or estate tax base; unlike the income tax charitable deduction, there are no percentage limits on the deductible amount. For estate tax purposes, the charitable deduction is limited to the value of the transferred property that is required to be included in the gross estate.[53] A charitable contribution of a partial interest in property, such as a remainder or future interest, generally is not deductible for gift or estate tax purposes.[54]

C. The Estate Tax

Overview

The Code imposes a tax on the transfer of the taxable estate of a decedent who is a citizen or resident of the United States.[55] The taxable estate is determined by deducting from the value of the decedent's gross estate any deductions provided for in the Code. After applying tax rates to determine a tentative amount of estate tax, certain credits are subtracted to determine estate tax liability.[56]

Because the estate tax shares a common unified credit (exemption) and tax rate table with the gift tax, the exemption amounts and tax rates are described together in Part III.B, above, along with certain other common features of these taxes.

Gross Estate

A decedent's gross estate includes, to the extent provided for in other sections of the Code, the date-of-death value of all of a decedent's property, real or personal, tangible or intangible, wherever situated.[57] In general, the value of property for this purpose is the fair market value of the property as of the date of the decedent's death, although an executor may elect to value certain property as of the date that is six months after the decedent's death (the alternate valuation date).[58]

The gross estate includes not only property directly owned by the decedent, but also other property in which the decedent had a beneficial interest at the time of his or her death.[59] The gross estate also includes certain transfers made by the decedent prior to his or her death, including: (1) certain gifts made within three years prior to the decedent's death;[60] (2) certain transfers of property in which the decedent retained a life estate;[61] (3) certain transfers taking effect at death;[62] and (4) revocable transfers.[63] In addition, the gross estate also includes property with respect to which the decedent had, at the time of death, a general power of appointment (generally, the right to determine who will have beneficial ownership).[64] The value of a life insurance policy on the decedent's life is included in the gross estate if the proceeds are payable to the decedent's estate or the decedent had incidents of ownership with respect to the policy at the time of his or her death.[65]

Deductions from the Gross Estate

A decedent's taxable estate is determined by subtracting from the value of the gross estate any deductions provided for in the Code.

Marital and Charitable Transfers

As described in Part III.B, above, transfers to a surviving spouse or to charity generally are deductible for estate tax purposes. The effect of the marital and charitable deductions generally is to remove assets transferred to a surviving spouse or to charity from the estate tax base.

State Death Taxes

An estate tax deduction is permitted for death taxes (*e.g.*, any estate, inheritance, legacy, or succession taxes) actually paid to any State or the District of Columbia, in respect of property included in the gross estate of the decedent.[66] Such State taxes must have been paid and claimed before the later of: (1) four years after the filing of the estate tax return; or (2) (a) 60 days after a decision of the U.S. Tax Court determining the estate tax liability becomes final, (b) the expiration of the period of extension to pay estate taxes over time under section 6166, or (c) the expiration of the period of limitations in which to file a claim for refund or 60 days after a decision of a court in which such refund suit has become final.

Other Deductions

A deduction is available for funeral expenses, estate administration expenses, and claims against the estate, including certain taxes.[67] A deduction also is available for uninsured casualty and theft losses incurred during the settlement of the estate.[68]

Credits against Tax

After accounting for allowable deductions, a gross amount of estate tax is computed. Estate tax liability is then determined by subtracting allowable credits from the gross estate tax.

Unified Credit

The most significant credit allowed for estate tax purposes is the unified credit, which is discussed in greater detail above.[69] For 2015, the value of the unified credit is $2,117,800, which has the effect of exempting $5.43 million in transfers from tax. The unified credit available at death is reduced by the amount of unified credit used to offset gift tax on gifts made during the decedent's life.

Other Credits

Estate tax credits also are allowed for: (1) gift tax paid on certain pre-1977 gifts (before the estate and gift tax computations were integrated);[70] (2) estate tax paid on certain prior transfers (to limit the estate tax burden when estate tax is imposed on transfers of the same property in two estates by reason of deaths in rapid succession);[71] and (3) certain foreign death taxes paid (generally, where the property is situated in a foreign country but included in the decedent's U.S. gross estate).[72]

Provisions Affecting Small and Family-Owned Businesses and Farms

Special-Use Valuation

An executor can elect to value for estate tax purposes certain "qualified real property" used in farming or another qualifying closely-held trade or business at its current-use value, rather than its fair market value.[73] The maximum reduction in value for such real property is $750,000 (adjusted for inflation occurring after 1997; the inflation-adjusted amount for 2015 is $1,100,000). In general, real property generally qualifies for special-use valuation only if (1) at least 50 percent of the adjusted value of the decedent's gross estate (including both real and personal property) consists of a farm or closely-held business property in the decedent's estate and (2) at least 25 percent of the adjusted value of the gross estate consists of farm or closely held business real property. In addition, the property must be used in a qualified use (*e.g.*, farming) by the decedent or a member of the decedent's family for five of the eight years before the decedent's death.

If, after a special-use valuation election is made, the heir who acquired the real property ceases to use it in its qualified use within 10 years of the decedent's death, an additional estate tax is imposed to recapture the entire estate-tax benefit of the special-use valuation.[74]

Installment Payment of Estate Tax for Closely Held Businesses

Under present law, the estate tax generally is due within nine months of a decedent's death. However, an executor generally may elect to pay estate tax attributable to an interest in a closely held business in two or more installments (but no more than 10).[75] An estate is eligible for payment of estate tax in installments if the value of the decedent's interest in a closely held business exceeds 35 percent of the decedent's adjusted gross estate (*i.e.*, the gross estate less certain deductions). If the election is made, the estate may defer payment of principal and pay only interest for the first five years, followed by up to 10 annual installments of principal and interest. This provision effectively extends the time for paying estate tax by 14 years from the original due date of the estate tax. A special two-percent interest rate applies to the amount of deferred estate tax attributable to the first $1 million (adjusted annually for inflation occurring after 1998; the inflation-adjusted amount for 2015 is $1,470,000) in taxable value of a closely held business. The interest rate applicable to the amount of estate tax attributable to the taxable value of the closely held business in excess of $1 million (adjusted for inflation) is equal to 45 percent of the rate applicable to underpayments of tax under section 6621 of the Code (*i.e.*, 45 percent of the Federal short-term rate plus three percentage points).[76] Interest paid on deferred estate taxes is not deductible for estate or income tax purposes.

D. The Gift Tax

Overview

The Code imposes a tax for each calendar year on the transfer of property by gift during such year by any individual, whether a resident or nonresident of the United States.[77] The amount of taxable gifts for a calendar year is determined by subtracting from the total amount of gifts made during the year: (1) the gift tax annual exclusion (described below); and (2) allowable deductions.

Gift tax for the current taxable year is determined by: (1) computing a tentative tax on the combined amount of all taxable gifts for the current and all prior calendar years using the common gift tax and estate tax rate table; (2) computing a tentative tax only on all prior-year gifts; (3) subtracting the tentative tax on prior-year gifts from the tentative tax computed for all years to arrive at the portion of the total tentative tax attributable to current-year gifts; and, finally, (4) subtracting the amount of unified credit not consumed by prior-year gifts.

Because the gift tax shares a common unified credit (exemption) and tax rate table with the estate tax, the exemption amounts and tax rates are described together in Part III.B, above, along with certain other common features of these taxes.

Transfers by Gift

The gift tax applies to a transfer by gift regardless of whether: (1) the transfer is made outright or in trust; (2) the gift is direct or indirect; or (3) the property is real or personal, tangible or intangible.[78] For gift tax purposes, the value of a gift of property is the fair market value of the property at the time of the gift.[79] Where property is transferred for less than full consideration, the amount by which the value of the property exceeds the value of the consideration is considered a gift and is included in computing the total amount of a taxpayer's gifts for a calendar year.[80]

For a gift to occur, a donor generally must relinquish dominion and control over donated property. For example, if a taxpayer transfers assets to a trust established for the benefit of his or her children, but retains the right to revoke the trust, the taxpayer may not have made a completed gift, because the taxpayer has retained dominion and control over the transferred assets. A completed gift made in trust, on the other hand, often is treated as a gift to the trust beneficiaries.

By reason of statute, certain transfers are not treated as transfers by gift for gift tax purposes. These include, for example, certain transfers for educational and medical purposes[81] and transfers to section 527 political organizations.[82]

Taxable Gifts

As stated above, the amount of a taxpayer's taxable gifts for the year is determined by subtracting from the total amount of the taxpayer's gifts for the year the gift tax annual exclusion and any available deductions.

Gift Tax Annual Exclusion

Under present law, donors of lifetime gifts are provided an annual exclusion of $14,000 per donee in 2015 (indexed for inflation from the 1997 annual exclusion amount of $10,000) for gifts of present interests in property during the taxable year.[83] If the non-donor spouse consents to split the gift with the donor spouse, then the annual exclusion is $28,000 per donee in 2015. In general, unlimited transfers between spouses are permitted without imposition of a gift tax. Special rules apply to the contributions to a qualified tuition program ("529 Plan") including an election to treat a contribution that exceeds the annual exclusion as a contribution made ratably over a five-year period beginning with the year of the contribution.[84]

Marital and Charitable Deductions

As described in Part III.B, above, transfers to a surviving spouse or to charity generally are deductible for gift tax purposes. The effect of the marital and charitable deductions generally is to remove assets transferred to a surviving spouse or to charity from the gift tax base.

E. The Generation-Skipping Transfer Tax

A generation-skipping transfer tax generally is imposed (in addition to the gift tax or the estate tax) on transfers, either directly or in trust or similar arrangement, to a "skip person" (*i.e.*, a beneficiary in a generation more than one generation below that of the transferor). Transfers subject to the generation-skipping transfer tax include direct skips, taxable terminations, and taxable distributions.

Exemption and Tax Rate

An exemption generally equal to the estate tax exemption amount ($5.43 million for 2015) is provided for each person making generation-skipping transfers. The exemption may be allocated by a transferor (or his or her executor) to transferred property, and in some cases is automatically allocated. The allocation of generation-skipping transfer tax exemption effectively reduces the tax rate on a generation-skipping transfer.

The tax rate on generation-skipping transfers is a flat rate of tax equal to the maximum estate and gift tax rate (40 percent) multiplied by the "inclusion ratio." The inclusion ratio with respect to any property transferred indicates the amount of "generation-skipping transfer tax exemption" allocated to a trust (or to property transferred in a direct skip) relative to the total value of property transferred.[85] If, for example, a taxpayer transfers $5 million in property to a trust and allocates $5 million of exemption to the transfer, the inclusion ratio is zero, and the applicable tax rate on any subsequent generation-skipping transfers from the trust is zero percent (40 percent multiplied by the inclusion ratio of zero). If, however, the taxpayer allocated only $2.5 million of exemption to the transfer, the inclusion ratio is 0.5, and the applicable tax rate on any subsequent generation-skipping transfers from the trust is 20 percent (40 percent multiplied by the inclusion ratio of 0.5). If the taxpayer allocates no exemption to the transfer, the inclusion ratio is one, and the applicable tax rate on any subsequent generation-skipping transfers from the trust is 40 percent (40 percent multiplied by the inclusion ratio of one).

Generation-Skipping Transfers

Generation-skipping transfer tax generally is imposed at the time of a generation-skipping transfer - a direct skip, a taxable termination, or a taxable distribution.

A direct skip is any transfer subject to estate or gift tax of an interest in property to a skip person. A skip person may be a natural person or certain trusts. All persons assigned to the second or more remote generation below the transferor are skip persons (*e.g.*, grandchildren and great-grandchildren). Trusts are skip persons if (1) all interests in the trust are held by skip persons, or (2) no person holds an interest in the trust and at no time after the transfer may a distribution (including distributions and terminations) be made to a non-skip person.

A taxable termination is a termination (by death, lapse of time, release of power, or otherwise) of an interest in property held in trust unless, immediately after such termination, a non-skip person has an interest in the property, or unless at no time after the termination may a distribution (including a distribution upon termination) be made from the trust to a skip person.

A taxable distribution is a distribution from a trust to a skip person (other than a taxable termination or direct skip). If a transferor allocates generation-skipping transfer tax exemption to a trust prior to the taxable distribution, generation-skipping transfer tax may be avoided.

F. Income Tax Basis in Property Received

In General

Gain or loss, if any, on the disposition of property is measured by the taxpayer's amount realized (*i.e.*, gross proceeds received) on the disposition, less the taxpayer's basis in such property. Basis generally represents a taxpayer's investment in property with certain adjustments required after acquisition. For example, basis is increased by the cost of capital improvements made to the property and decreased by depreciation deductions taken with respect to the property.

A gift or bequest of appreciated (or loss) property is not an income tax realization event for the transferor. The Code provides special rules for determining a recipient's basis in assets received by lifetime gift or from a decedent.

Basis in Property Received by Lifetime Gift

Under present law, property received from a donor of a lifetime gift generally takes a carryover basis. "Carryover basis" means that the basis in the hands of the donee is the same as it was in the hands of the donor. The basis of property transferred by lifetime gift also is increased, but not above fair market value, by any gift tax paid by the donor. The basis of a lifetime gift, however, generally cannot exceed the property's fair market value on the date of the gift. If a donor's basis in property is greater than the fair market value of the property on the date of the gift, then, for purposes of determining loss on a subsequent sale of the property, the donee's basis is the property's fair market value on the date of the gift.

Basis in Property Acquired from a Decedent

Property acquired from a decedent's estate generally takes a stepped-up basis. "Stepped-up basis" means that the basis of property acquired from a decedent's estate generally is the fair market value on the date of the decedent's death (or, if the alternate valuation date is elected, the earlier of six months after the decedent's death or the date the property is sold or distributed by the estate). Providing a fair market value basis eliminates the recognition of income on any appreciation of the property that occurred prior to the decedent's death and eliminates the tax benefit from any unrealized loss.

In community property states, a surviving spouse's one-half share of community property held by the decedent and the surviving spouse (under the community property laws of any State, U.S. possession, or foreign country) generally is treated as having passed from the decedent and, thus, is eligible for stepped-up basis. Thus, both the decedent's one-half share and the surviving spouse's one-half share are stepped up to fair market value. This rule applies if at least one-half of the whole of the community interest is includible in the decedent's gross estate.

Stepped-up basis treatment generally is denied to certain interests in foreign entities. Stock in a passive foreign investment company (including those for which a mark-to-market election has been made) generally takes a carryover basis, except that stock of a passive foreign investment company for which a decedent shareholder had made a qualified electing fund election is allowed a stepped-up basis. Stock owned by a decedent in a domestic international sales corporation (or former domestic international sales corporation) takes a stepped-up basis reduced by the amount (if any) which would have been included in gross income under section 995(c) as a dividend if the decedent had lived and sold the stock at its fair market value on the estate tax valuation date (*i.e.*, generally the date of the decedent's death unless an alternate valuation date is elected).

IV. Data and Economic Issues Relating to Estate and Gift Taxation

A. Background Data

Estates Subject to the Estate Tax

Table 2 details the percentage of decedents subject to the estate tax for selected years since 1935. The percentage of decedents liable for the estate tax grew throughout the postwar era reaching a peak in the mid-1970s. The substantial revision to the estate tax in the mid-1970s and subsequent further modifications in 1981 reduced the percentage of decedents liable for the estate tax to less than one percent in the late 1980s. The percentage of decedents liable for the estate tax increased from year to year from 1988 through 2000. The increases in the unified credit enacted in 2001 and 2010 (and made permanent in 2013) reduced substantially the percentage of decedents' estates liable for the estate tax.

The increasing percentage of decedents liable for estate tax in the period from 1940 through the mid-1970s and the similar increasing percentage from 1989 to 2000 are the result of the interaction of three factors: a fixed nominal exemption; the effect of price inflation on asset values; and real economic growth (and, correspondingly, real wealth growth). Prior to 2011, the amount of wealth exempt from the Federal estate tax had always been expressed at a fixed nominal value. If the general price level in the economy rises from one year to the next and asset values rise to reflect this inflation, the "nominal" value of each individual's wealth will increase. With a fixed nominal exemption, annual increases in the price level will imply that more individuals will have a nominal wealth that exceeds the tax threshold. Alternatively stated, inflation diminishes the real, inflation-adjusted, value of wealth that is exempted by a nominal exemption. Thus, even if no one individual's real wealth increased, more individuals would be subject to the estate tax. This interaction between inflation and a fixed nominal exemption largely explains the pattern in Table 2.[86] The fixed nominal exemption was increased effective for 1977, again between 1982 and 1987, and a series of increases was enacted in 2001, 2010, and 2013. Prior to 1977 and from 1987 through 2001, the exemption was little changed while the economy experienced general price inflation.

Table 2. Number of Taxable Estate Tax Returns Filed as a Percentage of Deaths, Selected Years, 1935-2013

		Taxable estate tax returns filed[1]	
Year	**Deaths**	**Number**	**Percent of deaths**
1935	1,172,245	8,655	0.74
1940	1,237,186	12,907	1.04
1945	1,239,713	13,869	1.12
1950	1,304,343	17,411	1.33
1955	1,379,826	25,143	1.82
1961	1,548,665	45,439	2.93
1966	1,727,240	67,404 [2]	3.90
1970	1,796,940	93,424 [2]	5.20
1973	1,867,689	120,761 [2]	6.47
1977	1,819,107	139,115 [2]	7.65
1982	1,897,820	41,620 [2,3]	2.19
1984	1,968,128	31,507 [2,3]	1.60
1986	2,105,361	23,731	1.13
1988	2,167,999	18,948	0.87
1990 [4]	2,148,463	23,104	1.08
1992 [4]	2,175,613	27,397	1.26
1994 [4]	2,278,994	31,918	1.40
1996 [4]	2,314,690	37,711	1.63
1998 [4]	2,337,256	47,475	2.03
2000 [4]	2,403,351	52,000	2.16
2002 [4]	2,443,387	45,018	1.84
2004 [4]	2,397,615	31,329	1.31
2006 [4]	2,426,264	22,798	0.94

		Taxable estate tax returns filed[1]	
Year	Deaths	Number	Percent of deaths
2008 [4]	2,471,984	17,144	0.69
2010 [4]	2,468,435	6,711	0.27
2011 [4]	2,515,458	1,480	0.06
2012 [4]	2,543,279	3,738	0.15
2013 [4]	2,596,993	4,687	0.18

[1] Estate tax returns need not be filed in the year of the decedent's death.

[2] Not strictly comparable with pre-1966 data. For later years the estate tax after credits was the basis for determining taxable returns. For prior years, the basis was the estate tax before credits.

[3] Although the filing requirement was for gross estates in excess of $225,000 for 1982 deaths, $275,000 for 1983 deaths, and $325,000 for 1984 deaths, the data are limited to gross estates of $300,000 or more.

[4] Taxable estate data from 1989-2013 are from Internal Revenue Service, *Statistics of Income*.

Sources: Joseph A. Pechman, *Federal Tax Policy* (Washington: Brookings Institution), 1987; Internal Revenue Service, *Statistics of Income*; and U.S. National Center for Health Statistics.

However, even now that the exemption is modified annually to reflect general price inflation, one would still expect to see the percentage of decedents liable for estate tax rise because of the third factor, real growth. If the economy is experiencing real growth per capita, it must be accumulating capital.[87] Accumulated capital is the tax base of the estate tax. Thus, real growth can lead to more individuals having real wealth above any given fixed real exempt amount.[88]

Revenues from the Estate, Gift, and Generation-Skipping Taxes

Table 3 provides summary statistics of the estate and gift tax for selected years from 1940 through 2014. Total estate and gift receipts include taxes paid for estate, gift, and generation-skipping transfer taxes as well as payments made as the result of IRS audits.

Between 1990 and 1999, transfer tax receipts averaged double-digit rates of growth. There are three possible reasons for the rapid growth in these receipts. First, because neither the amount of wealth that was exempt from transfer taxes nor the tax rates were indexed for inflation, as explained above, an increasing number of persons were subject to estate and gift taxes. Second, the substantial increase in value in the stock market during the decade of the 1990s increased the value of estates that would have already been taxable, and increased the number of taxable estates. For example, the Dow Jones

Industrial Average ended 1989 at approximately 2,750 and ended 1999 at approximately 11,000. A substantial portion of the wealth in taxable estates consists of publicly traded stocks. Because the value of this component of wealth more than tripled during the decade, one would expect brisk growth in estate tax receipts from this alone.

Table 3. Revenue from the Estate, Gift, and Generation-Skipping Transfer Taxes, Selected Fiscal Years, 1940-2014

Year	**Revenues ($ Millions)**	**Percentage of total Federal receipts**
1940	353	5.4
1945	637	1.4
1950	698	1.8
1955	924	1.4
1960	1,606	1.7
1965	2,716	2.3
1970	3,644	1.9
1975	4,611	1.7
1980	6,389	1.2
1985	6,422	0.9
1990	11,500	1.1
1995	14,763	1.1
2000	29,010	1.4
2005	24,764	1.1
2006	27,877	1.2
2007	26,044	1.0
2008	28,844	1.1
2009	23,482	1.1
2010	18,885	0.9
2011	7,399	0.3
2012	13.973	0.6
2013	18,912	0.7
2014	19,300	0.6

Sources: *Budget of the United States Government, Fiscal Year 2016: Historical Tables*, Tables 2.1 and 2.5, accessed at www.whitehouse.gov /omb/budget /Historicals.

Finally, the unlimited marital deduction included in the 1981 Act delayed the payment of estate tax, in most cases, until the surviving spouse died. As a result, married taxpayers who died during the 1980s were able to reduce estate tax liability by claiming an unlimited marital deduction for transfers to a surviving spouse. This resulted in an increase in estate tax receipts during the decade of the 1990s, when a significant number of such surviving spouses died and paid estate tax on assets acquired from an earlier-deceased spouse.[89]

On the other hand, the 1997, 2001, 2010 and 2013 Acts included provisions that would be expected to reduce the number of estates subject to the estate tax. As explained above, the exemption equivalent amount provided by the unified credit increased to $3.5 million in 2009 and $5 million in 2010.[90] The $5 million figure is indexed for inflation for inflation for years after 2011 and stands at $5.43 million for 2015. The average rate of increase in the exemption amount exceeds the rate of inflation. As explained above, increases in the real value of the unified credit generally would be expected to reduce the number of estates subject to tax. The 1997 Act also provided an additional exemption for certain qualified family-owned business interests and a partial exclusion from the estate tax of the value of land subject to certain conservation easements. While the exemption for qualified family-owned business is no longer operable, these changes reduced the number of estates that would be expected to be subject to tax between 1997 and the present.

Table 4. Projections of Taxable Estates and Receipts from Estate, Gift, and Generation-Skipping Transfer Taxes, 2015-2024

Year	Exemption value of unified credit	Number of taxable estates	Percent of deaths	Receipts ($ billions)
2015	$5,430,000	5,400	0.2	21.5
2016	$5,490,000	5,400	0.2	21.9
2017	$5,600,000	5,400	0.2	22.5
2018	$5,730,000	5,400	0.2	23.3
2019	$5,860,000	5,400	0.2	24.2
2020	$6,000,000	5,500	0.2	25.0
2021	$6,140,000	5,500	0.2	26.0
2022	$6,290,000	5,500	0.2	26.8
2023	$6,450,000	5,500	0.2	27.6
2024	$6,600,000	5,500	0.2	28.4

Source: Joint Committee on Taxation staff estimates and calculations based on U.S. Census Bureau estimates of deaths from National Population Projections: Downloadable Files, Table 3, available at www.census.gov/population/projections /data/national/2014/downloadablefiles.html.

Table 4 shows the Joint Committee on Taxation staff present-law estimate of revenues from the estate, gift, and generation-skipping transfer taxes resulting from transfers in calendar years 2015-2024. These estimates are based on the December 2014 baseline forecast for estate, gift, and generation-skipping transfer taxes supplied by the Congressional Budget Office. Table 4 also reports the Joint Committee on Taxation staff estimates of annual taxable estates and calculations of the percentage of all deaths that taxable estates will represent.

B. Economic Issues Related to Transfer Taxation

Taxes on Income versus Taxes on Wealth

Income taxes, payroll taxes, and excise and other consumption taxes generally tax economic activity as it occurs. Income and consumption represent ongoing, current economic activity by the taxpayer.[91] Estate and gift taxes are levied on the transfer of accumulated wealth. Accumulated wealth does not result from any ongoing, current economic activity.[92] Wealth depends upon previous economic activity either by the current wealth holder or other individuals. For example, current wealth can result from accumulated saving from income or from bequests received.

Taxes on wealth are not directly comparable to taxes on income. Because wealth is the accumulation of flows of saving over a period of years, taxes on wealth are not directly comparable to taxes on income or consumption which may represent only current, rather than accumulated, economic activity. For example, assume that a taxpayer receives wage income of $10,000 per year, saves all of this income, and the savings earn an annual return of five percent. At the end of five years, the accumulated value of the taxpayer's investments would be $58,019. Assume that the wealth is transferred at the end of the fifth year. If a 10-percent tax were imposed on wage income, one would conclude that a burden of $1,000 was imposed annually. If a 10-percent tax were imposed on the transfer of wealth, one might conclude that a burden of $5,801.90 was imposed at the end of the fifth year. If, after paying the wage tax, the taxpayer had invested the remaining $9,000 each year to earn five percent, the taxpayer's holding would be $52,217.10 at the end of five years. This is the same value that would remain under the wealth tax ($58,019.00 less $5,801.90). Thus, it is misleading to say that the burden of the wage tax is $1,000 in each year while the burden of the transfer tax is $5,801.90 in only the fifth year. It may be more appropriate to allocate the transfer tax burden over the years in which the capital income was earned.[93]

Wealth Taxes, Saving, and Investment

Taxes on accumulated wealth are taxes on the stock of capital held by the taxpayer. As a tax on capital, issues similar to those that arise in analyzing any tax on the income from capital arise. In particular, while economic analysis concludes that in the long run owners of domestic capital are more easily able to escape some of the burden of the tax such that a tax on capital is at least partially passed on to labor, there is no consensus among economists on the extent to which the incidence of taxes on the income from capital is borne by owners of capital in the form of reduced returns, or whether reduced returns cause investors to save less and provide less capital to workers, thereby reducing wages in the long run.[94] A related issue is to what extent individuals respond to increases (or decreases) in the after-tax return to investments by decreasing (or increasing) their saving. Again, there is no consensus in either the empirical or theoretical economics literature regarding the responsiveness of saving to after-tax returns on investment.[95]

Some economists believe that an individual's bequest motives are important to understanding saving behavior and aggregate capital accumulation. If estate and gift taxes alter the bequest motive, they may change the tax burdens of taxpayers other than the decedent and his or her heirs.[96] It is an open question whether the bequest motive is an economically important explanation of taxpayer saving behavior and level of the capital stock. For example, theoretical analysis suggests that the bequest motive may account for between 15 and 70 percent of the United States' capital stock.[97] Others believe the bequest motive is not important in national capital formation,[98] and empirical analysis of the existence of a bequest motive has not led to a consensus.[99] Theoretically, it is an open question whether estate and gift taxes encourage or discourage saving, and there has been limited empirical analysis of this specific issue.[100] By raising the after-tax cost of leaving a bequest, a more expansive estate tax may discourage potential transferors from accumulating the assets necessary to make a bequest. On the other hand, a taxpayer who wants to leave a bequest of a certain net size might save more in response to estate taxation to meet that goal. For example, some individuals purchase additional life insurance to have sufficient funds to pay the estate tax without disposing of other assets in their estate.

Wealth Taxes and Labor Supply

As people become wealthier, they have an incentive to consume more of everything, including leisure time. Some, therefore, suggest that, by reducing the amount of wealth transferrable to heirs, transfer taxes may reduce labor supply of the parent, although it may increase labor supply of the heir. Over 120 years ago, Andrew Carnegie opined that "the parent who leaves his son enormous wealth generally deadens the talents and energies of the son, and tempts him to lead a less useful and less worthy life than he otherwise would . . ."[101] Furthermore, the estate tax could increase work effort of heirs as the benefits of the special-use valuation, and the exclusion for qualified family-owned business interests will be lost and recaptured if the assets fail to remain in a qualified use. While, in theory, increases in wealth should reduce labor supply, empirically economists have found the magnitude of these effects to be small.[102] In addition, the estate tax also could distort, in either direction, the labor supply of the transferor if it distorts his or her decision to make a bequest.

Wealth Taxes, the Distribution of Wealth, and Fairness

Some suggest that, in addition to their role in producing Federal revenue, Federal transfer taxes may help prevent an increase in the concentration of wealth. Overall, there are relatively few analyses of the distribution of wealth holdings in the economic literature.[103] Conventional economic wisdom holds that the Great Depression of the 1930s and World War II substantially reduced the concentration of wealth in the United States, and that there had been no substantial change at least through the 1980s. More recently, some economists have studied the distribution of wealth and noted an increase in wealth concentration in the last several decades.[104] Most analysts assign no role to tax policy in the reduction in wealth concentration that occurred between 1930 and 1945. Nor has any analyst been able to quantify what role tax policy might have played since World War II.[105]

The income tax does not tax all sources of income. Some suggest that by serving as a "backstop" for income that escapes income taxation, transfer taxes may help promote overall fairness of the U.S. tax system.[106] Still others counter that to the extent that much wealth was accumulated with after-(income)-tax dollars, as an across-the-board tax on wealth, transfer taxes tax more than just those monies that may have escaped the income tax. In addition, depending upon the incidence of such taxes, it is difficult to make an assessment regarding the contribution of transfer taxes to the overall fairness of the U.S. tax system.

Even if transfer taxes are believed to be borne by the owners of the assets subject to tax, an additional conceptual difficulty is whether the tax is borne by the generation of the transferor or the generation of the transferee. The design of the gift tax illustrates this conceptual difficulty. A gift tax is assessed on the transferor of taxable gifts. Assume, for example, a mother makes a gift of $1 million to her son and incurs a gift tax liability of $400,000. From one perspective, the gift tax could be said to have reduced the mother's current economic well-being by $400,000. However, it is possible that, in the absence of the gift tax, the mother would have given her son $1.4 million, so that the gift tax has reduced the son's economic well-being by $400,000. It also is possible that the economic well-being of both was reduced. Of course, distinctions between the donor and recipient generations may not be important to assessing the fairness of transfer taxes if both the donor and recipient have approximately the same income.[107]

Federal Estate Taxation and Charitable Bequests

The two unlimited exclusions under the Federal estate tax are for bequests to a surviving spouse and for bequests to a charity. Because charitable bequests are deductible against the estate tax, the after-tax cost of a charitable bequest is lower than the after-tax cost of a transfer to an heir who is not a spouse.[108] Economists refer to this incentive as the "price" or "substitution effect." In short, the price effect says that if something is made cheaper, people will do more of it. Some analysts have suggested that the charitable estate tax deduction creates a strong incentive to make charitable bequests and that changes in Federal estate taxation could alter the amount of funds that flow to charitable purposes. The decision to make a charitable bequest arises not only from the incentive effect of a charitable bequest's deductibility, or "tax price," but also from what economists call the "wealth effect." Generally the wealthier an individual is, the more likely he or she is to make a charitable bequest, and the larger the bequest will be. Because the estate tax diminishes the amount of wealth available to an heir, the wealth effect would suggest repeal of the estate tax could increase charitable bequests.

A number of studies have examined the effects of estate taxes on charitable bequests. Most of these studies have concluded that, after controlling for the size of the estate and other factors, deductibility of charitable bequests encourages taxpayers to provide charitable bequests.[109] Some analysts interpret these findings as implying that reductions in estate taxation could lead to a reduction in funds flowing into the charitable sector. This is not necessarily the case, however. Some charitable bequests may substitute for lifetime giving to charity, in part to take advantage of the greater value of the charitable deduction under the estate tax than under the income tax that results from the lower marginal income tax rates and limitations on annual lifetime giving. If this is the case, reductions in the estate tax could lead to increased charitable giving during the taxpayer's life. On the other hand, some analysts have suggested that a more sophisticated analysis is required recognizing that a taxpayer may choose among bequests to charity, bequests to heirs, lifetime gifts to charity, and lifetime gifts to heirs and recognizing that lifetime gifts reduce the future taxable estate and consumption. In this more complex framework, reductions in estate taxation could reduce lifetime charitable gifts.[110]

Federal Transfer Taxes and Complexity

Critics of Federal transfer taxes document that these taxes create incentives to engage in avoidance activities. Some of these avoidance activities involve complex legal structures and can be expensive to create. Incurring these costs, while ultimately profitable from the donors' and donees' perspective, is socially wasteful because time, effort, and financial resources are spent that lead to no increase in productivity. Such costs represent an efficiency loss to the economy in addition to whatever distorting effects Federal transfer taxes may have on other economic choices such as saving and labor supply discussed above. For example, in the case of family-owned businesses, such activities may impose an ongoing cost by creating a business structure to reduce transfer tax burdens that may not be the most efficient business structure for the operation of the business. Reviewing more complex legal arrangements increases the administrative cost of the Internal Revenue Service. There is disagreement among analysts regarding the magnitude of the costs of avoidance activities.[111] It is difficult to measure the extent to which any such costs incurred are undertaken from tax avoidance motives as opposed to succession planning or other motives behind gifts and bequests.

Alternatives to the Current U.S. Estate Tax System

Some argue that Congress should consider an alternative structure for taxing transfers of wealth. The choice of one form of wealth transfer tax system over another necessarily will involve tradeoffs among efficiency, equity, administrability, and other factors. A determination whether one system is preferable to another could be made on the basis of each system's relative success in achieving one or a majority of these goals, without sacrificing excessively the achievement of the others. Alternatively, such a determination could be made based on which system provides the best mix of efficiency, equity, and administrability.

The United States, State governments, and foreign jurisdictions tax transfers of wealth in many different ways. Some wealth transfer tax systems, for example, impose a tax on the transferor. Such systems include the U.S. estate and gift tax system, which imposes a gift tax on certain gratuitous lifetime transfers, an estate tax on a decedent's estate, and a generation skipping transfer tax on certain transfers that skip generations. Another approach that involves imposition of a tax on a transferor is a "deemed-realization" approach, under which a gratuitous transfer is treated as a realization event and the gain on transferred assets, if any, generally is taxed to the transferor as capital gain.

Other wealth transfer tax systems tax the transferee of a gift or bequest.[112] Such systems include inheritance (or "accessions") tax systems, under which a tax is imposed on the recipient of a gratuitous transfer. Some jurisdictions do not impose a separate tax, but instead treat receipts of gifts or bequests as gross income of the recipient under the income tax system (an "income inclusion approach").

Regardless of whether the tax is imposed on the transferor or the transferee, some commentators assert that the real economic burden of any approach to taxing transfers of wealth falls on the recipients, because the amount received effectively is reduced by the amount of tax paid by the transferor or realized by the transferee.[113] Some commentators argue that systems that impose a tax based on the circumstances of the transferee –such as an inheritance tax or an income inclusion approach – are more effective in encouraging dispersal of wealth among a greater number of transferees and potentially to lower-income beneficiaries. Others assert that such systems promote fairness in the tax system. However, the extent to which one form of transfer tax system in practice is more effective than another in achieving these goals is not clear.

Wealth transfer tax systems other than an estate tax also may present benefits or additional challenges in administration or compliance. Inheritance taxes or income inclusion systems, for example, may reduce the need for costly tax planning in the case of certain transfers between spouses. At the same time, to the extent such systems are effective in encouraging distributions to multiple recipients in lower tax brackets, they may be susceptible to abuse such as through the use of multiple nominal recipients as conduits for a transfer intended for a single beneficiary.

Wealth Taxes and Small Business

Regardless of any potential effect on aggregate saving, the scope and design of the transfer tax system may affect the composition of investment. In particular, some observers note that the transfer tax system may impose special cash flow burdens on small or family-owned businesses. They note that if a family has a substantial proportion of its wealth invested in one enterprise, the need to pay estate taxes may force heirs to liquidate all or part of the enterprise or to encumber the business with debt to meet the estate tax liability. If the business is sold, while the assets generally do not cease to exist and remain a productive part of the economy, the share of business represented by small or family-owned businesses may be diminished by the estate tax. If the business borrows to meet estate tax liability, the business's cash flow may be strained. There is some evidence that many businesses may be constrained in the amount of funds they can borrow. If businesses are constrained, they may reduce the amount of investment in the business and this would be a market inefficiency.[114] One study suggests that reduction in estate taxes may have a positive effect on the survival of an entrepreneur's business.[115]

Others argue that potential deleterious effects of the estate tax on investment by small or family-owned businesses are limited. The basic exclusion amount is $5.43 million per decedent for decedents dying in 2015. As a result, small business owners can obtain an effective exclusion of up to $10.86 million per married couple for decedents dying in 2015, and other legitimate tax planning can further reduce the burden on such enterprises. For example, lifetime gifts to heirs of interests in the closely held business reduce the eventual estate tax liability attributable to business assets. Alternatively, lifetime gifts of cash or securities may provide funds to heirs to meet some or all of an estate tax liability that may be attributable to closely held business assets. Some analysis questions whether, in practice, small businesses need to liquidate operating assets to meet estate tax liabilities. Also, as described above, sections 2032A and 6166 are provided to reduce the impingement on small business cash flow that may result from an estate tax liability. Others have argued that estate tax returns report a small fraction of the value of decedents' estates thereby mitigating any special burden that the estate tax may impose on small business.[116]

It is difficult to assess the degree to which estate tax impedes the survival and future growth of a closely held small business. Any tax payment reduces funds available to the heirs, but at the choice of the heirs, some or all of the reduction in funds could come from reduced personal consumption by the heirs rather than by reduced future business investment. Similarly, rather than reduce business investment, the decedent may have chosen to reduce his or her personal consumption to assure that the business would be adequately funded after payment of any transfer taxes.

Examination of 2001 Data

A study of estate returns of persons who died in 2001 shows that many estates that claimed benefits under sections 2032A, 2057, or 6166 held liquid assets nearly sufficient to meet all debts against the estate and that only 2.4 percent of estates that reported closely held business assets and agricultural assets elected the deferral of tax under section 6166.[117] This study uses detailed estate tax return data to calculate a liquidity ratio, the ratio of liquid assets (cash, cash management accounts, State and local bonds, Federal government bonds, publicly traded stock, and insurance on the life of the decedent) to the sum of the net estate tax plus mortgages and liens. A liquidity ratio of one or more implies that the estate has liquid assets sufficient to pay the net estate tax plus pay off all mortgages and liens. The study found that in 2001, on average, this ratio exceeded three for estates of less than $2.5 million claiming benefits of the special deduction for qualified family owned business assets or the section 2032A special use valuation.[118] This means that, on average such estates had $3 in liquid assets for every $1 of estate tax liability and mortgage and lien. The study found that for estates of less than $2.5 million electing deferral of tax, the average liquidity ratio was slightly larger than one.[119]

A liquidity ratio of one or more suggests that closely held business assets need not be sold, nor need a loan be incurred, to pay the estate tax. While the existence of liquid assets can insure that core business assets are unencumbered by the estate tax, the business's ability to function could be adversely affected by the reduction in liquid assets. Ongoing businesses need liquid assets in order to purchase raw materials, pay labor, finance expansion, and engage in other routine business activities. The greater the liquidity ratio is above one, the less likely that on-going business needs are impaired. The study found that generally all estates claiming special use valuations had an average liquidity ratio of at least one. For larger estates claiming benefits of the special deduction for qualified family owned business assets or deferral of tax, liquidity ratios averaged 0.5 or more.[120] While a liquidity ratio of less than one suggests that it is likely that closely held business assets would be impaired by the estate tax liability, it is important to remember the limitations of the estate tax data. These data do not show pre-death estate planning transfers of assets to the heirs who might ultimately be running the business. For example, the purchase of life insurance by the heirs is a common planning technique to insure that business assets need not be sold to meet estate tax liabilities. Insurance amounts paid on the death of the decedent to a person other than the estate are not included as liquid assets for the purpose of computing the liquidity ratios reported in the study.[121]

Examination of 2011 Data

A limitation of the study discussed above is that it reports the average liquidity ratio. If there is substantial variation in the way owners of closely held business assets manage their affairs, an average does not provide sufficient detail as to the extent to which the estate tax may or may not be thought to impair the continuity of closely held businesses upon the death of an owner.

In Tables 5 though 7, below, the staff of the Joint Committee on Taxation replicates the computation of the liquidity ratio on the 2011 estates with farm assets and closely held stock, but in addition to reporting the overall average liquidity ratio, the tables report average liquidity ratios from the second and ninth deciles of the distribution of such returns. Specifically, Tables 5 and 6 report liquidity ratios for 2011 estates that included farm property as an asset in the estate (1,275 estates) and estates that included farm property that claimed the special use valuation (58 estates). Table 5 reports liquidity ratios for all such estates, while Table 6 reports liquidity ratios for those estates with an estate tax liability ("taxable estates"). The first row reports the average liquidity ratio of all 2011 estates that included farm property as an asset in the estate and all 2011 estates that included farm property that also claimed the special use valuation. For this purpose, the JCT staff assigns a zero liquidity ratio to estates with no tax liability.[122] In order to provide another measure of liquidity, the JCT staff also reports the percentage of estates that are "well funded." A well-funded estate is an estate whose liquidity ratio is at least one or which has no tax liability. The JCT staff ranks and numbers all estates with farm property and all estates with farm property claiming a special use valuation from the estate with the lowest liquidity ratio to the estate with the highest liquidity ratio. The second decile of estates with farm property is contained within the first 689 estates with a liquidity ratio of zero; the second decile of estates with farm property claiming the special use valuation is contained within the first 23 estates with a liquidity ratio of zero. Likewise the ninth deciles are estates with farm property numbered 1,020 to 1,148 and for estates with farm property claiming the special use valuation numbered 46 to 52. The second row reports the average liquidity ratio for the second decile, the third row reports the median liquidity ratio, and the fourth row reports the average liquidity ratio for the ninth decile. The fifth row presents the percentage of estates that are well funded.

Table 5. Liquidity Ratios for Estates with Farm Property and Estates with Farm Property Claiming Benefits under Sec. 2032A 2011 Decedents

	All Estates including Farm Property	Estates including Farm Property and claiming special-use valuation
Average liquidity ratio	3.3	2.6
Average liquidity ratio of the second decile	0	0
Median liquidity ratio	0	0.7
Average liquidity ratio of the ninth decile	4.9	4.2
Percent of estates that are well-funded	89	84

Table 6. Liquidity Ratios for Taxable Estates with Farmland and Estates with Farmland Claiming Benefits Under Sec. 2032A 2011 Decedents

	All Estates including Farm Property	Estates including Farm Property and claiming special-use valuation
Average liquidity ratio	7.2	4.5
Average liquidity ratio of the second decile	0.6	0.5
Median liquidity ratio	2.8	1.7
Average liquidity ratio of the ninth decile	10.4	8.8
Percentage of estates that are well-funded	77	73

Tables 5 and 6 present rather similar results. The majority of estates with farm property and those claiming benefits of section 2032A have either a liquidity ratio of zero (meaning no estate tax liability) or a liquidity ratio of one or more. In Table 6 the average liquidity ratio in the second decile of estates with farm property is less than one. That is, the estate's estate tax liability and other debts exceed the value of liquid assets contained in the estate. For taxable estates claiming the special-use valuation the liquidity ratio of half of the estates exceeds 1.7. These data suggest that most estates with farm property and estates that claim the special use valuation generally are not directly impaired by an estate tax liability. In 2011, these estates generally included sufficient liquid assets to pay the estate tax, if any, without necessitating a sale of farmland.[123]

In 2011, an estate could claim benefits under section 2032A and reduce the value of the estate below the threshold at which any estate tax would be liable. Unlike section 2032A, section 6166 is only beneficial to an estate if the estate has an estate tax liability after application of the provision. The second column of Table 7 below reports liquidity ratios for estates with closely held stock. The third column of Table 7 reports liquidity ratios for those estates that defer payment of the estate tax liability under section 6166. Comparison of column three to column two indicates that estates that use the deferred payment of section 6166 have lower liquidity ratios than all estates that include closely held stock. Such a result is consistent with the purpose of section 6166, to provide deferral when sale of closely held business assets might otherwise be necessary to meet an estate tax obligation.

Table 7. Liquidity Ratios for Estates with Closely Held Stock and Estates Electing to Defer Payment Under Sec. 6166 2011 Decedents[1]

	All estates including closely held business assets	**All estates including closely held business assets and electing deferral of tax liability under sec. 6166**
Average liquidity ratio	10.1	0.5
Average liquidity ratio of the second decile	0	0. 1
Median liquidity ratio	0	0.4
Average liquidity ratio of the ninth decile	3.7	0.9
Percent of estates that are well-funded	89	13

[1] The total number of estates with closely held stock was 2,745. Of those estates, 88 made an election under section 6166.

More Recent Data

As described previously, several Code provisions may reduce the burden of the estate tax borne by small or family-owned businesses. Table 8,[124] below, presents data from estate tax returns filed in 2013 on the utilization of these provisions in comparison to all estate tax returns filed. In 2013, among estates with a positive estate tax liability, approximately three percent elected deferral under section 6166. Among with a positive estate tax liability, approximately 1.4 percent claimed a special use valuation under section 2032A.

Table 8. Estates Claiming a Special Use Valuation or Electing Deferral of Tax Liability, Returns Filed in 2013

Item	All Estates
Number of returns filed	10,568
Number of taxable returns	4,687
Number of returns claiming a special use valuation under sec. 2032A	128
Number of taxable returns claiming a special use valuation under sec. 2032A	65
Number of returns making sec. 6166 election	147
Number of returns claiming a special use valuation and making sec. 6166 election	19

Source: JCT staff tabulations from Statistics of Income data.

Table 9. Closely Held Stock in Estate Tax Returns Filed in 2013

Item	All Estates
Number of returns filed	10,568
Total gross estate (millions of dollars)	138,699
Value of closely held stock millions of dollars)	11,350
Value of closely held stock as a percentage of total gross estate	8.2%
Number of estates with closely held stock	3,115
Number of estates with closely held stock as a percentage of all returns filed	29.5%
Total gross estate of those estates with closely held stock (millions of dollars)	59,823
Number of estates with closely held stock and claiming benefits of secs. 2032A or 6166	126
Value of closely held stock as a percentage of the taxable gross estate of estates claiming benefits of secs. 2032A or 6166	52.4%
Number of estates with closely held stock not claiming benefits of secs. 2032A or 6166	2,989
Value of closely held stock as a percentage of the taxable gross estate of estates not claiming benefits of secs. 2032A or 6166	16.6%

Source: JCT staff tabulations from Statistics of Income data.

Table 9,[125] below, reports data on the extent to which estates are made up of closely held stock or business interests. The data show that approximately 30 percent of estate tax returns filed in 2013 reported some holdings of closely held stock. For estates claiming the tax benefits provided by section 2032A or 6166, the holdings of closely held stock comprised more than half of the taxable estate. For estates holding closely held stock, but not claiming the tax benefits provided by section 2032A or 6166, closely held stock represented about one-sixth of the taxable gross estate on average.

V. Selected Proposals to Modify the Taxation of Wealth Transfers

A. Overview

Lawmakers and the Administration have offered numerous proposals to modify the taxation of wealth transfers. This section describes recent proposals to: (1) repeal the estate and generation-skipping transfer taxes; (2) expand the taxation of wealth transfers by decreasing exemption amounts and increasing tax rates; (3) expand the transfer tax base; and (4) impose a new tax on the transfer of built-in gains at the time of a gift or upon a decedent's death.

B. Proposals to Repeal the Estate and Generation-Skipping Transfer Taxes

In recent decades, several lawmakers and commentators have proposed repealing the estate and generation-skipping transfer taxes outright. Proponents sometimes argue that repeal is necessary in part because the transfer tax system imposes special cash flow burdens on small or family-owned businesses and farms. Opponents sometimes argue that, in addition to producing Federal revenue, the transfer tax system helps limit concentrations of wealth. These and other considerations are discussed in Part IV.B, above.

As is discussed in Part II, above, EGTRRA provided for the gradual phase-out of the estate and generation-skipping transfer taxes, followed by repeal of those taxes for only one year, *i.e.*, for decedents dying and generation-skipping transfers made during 2010. This temporary repeal regime, however, ultimately was replaced with the present-law transfer tax rules.

More recently, Representative Kevin Brady introduced a bill to repeal the estate and generation-skipping transfer taxes.[126] The "Death Tax Repeal Act of 2015" generally would terminate the estate and generation-skipping transfer taxes for decedents dying and generation-skipping transfers made after the date of enactment. The bill would retain the gift tax with the present-law exemption amount ($5 million, indexed for inflation occurring after 2011) and a top gift tax rate of 35 percent.[127] Unlike the temporary repeal under EGTRRA, the bill would not modify the present-law rules for determining the basis of assets acquired by gift or bequest. Therefore, assets acquired from a decedent generally would be stepped up to fair market value under section 1014.

C. Proposals to Reduce Exemption Amounts and Increase Tax Rates

Other recent proposals would expand the reach of the present-law wealth transfer taxes by reducing exemption amounts, increasing tax rates, and broadening the transfer tax base. Arguments in favor of or in opposition to such proposals generally are the inverse of arguments regarding repeal of some or all of the wealth transfer taxes: proponents sometimes argue that a more robust transfer tax system will produce additional revenue and help prevent further concentrations of wealth, while opponents sometimes argue that expanding the estate tax will harm owners of small businesses and farms. These and other considerations are discussed in greater detail in Part IV.B, above.

The Administration's Fiscal Year 2016 budget proposal, for example, generally would put 2009-law estate and gift tax parameters back into place, but would retain the present-law rules regarding portability between spouses of unused exemption.[128] The exemption amount would be $3.5 million for estate and generation-skipping transfer tax purposes and $1 million for gift tax purposes, with neither amount being indexed for inflation. The top estate and gift tax rate would be 45 percent.

The "Sensible Estate Tax Act of 2014," introduced by Representative Jim McDermott, similarly would modify the present-law transfer tax rules by reducing the exemption amount and increasing the applicable tax rates.[129] Among other changes, the bill would reduce the exemption amount for estate, gift, and generation-skipping transfer tax purposes to $1 million, indexed for inflation occurring after 2000. The bill also would increase the top marginal tax rate to 55 percent and provide for inflation indexing of the rate bracket cut-off points (*i.e.*, the stated dollar amount above which each marginal rate included in the rate table applies).

D. Proposals to Expand the Transfer Tax Base

Other recent proposals seek to expand the transfer tax base by closing perceived loopholes that allow for avoidance of estate, gift, or generation-skipping transfer tax. The Administration's 2016 Fiscal Year budget includes several such proposals, and Members of Congress have included some of these proposals in introduced bills. The subsections below describe three examples of proposals to broaden the transfer tax base.

Require a Minimum Term for Grantor Retained Annuity Trusts

One such proposal, for example, would modify the tax rules for grantor retained annuity trusts ("GRATs"), which often are used to minimize transfer tax liability. In a GRAT structure, the grantor generally retains a right to receive a stream of payments for a period of time, after which the assets that remain in the GRAT are distributed to the remainder beneficiaries, often heirs of the grantor. When the grantor funds the trust, he is treated as making a taxable gift to the remainder beneficiaries equal to the value of the remainder interest. That value is determined by deducting from the total value of assets transferred to the trust the value of the retained annuity interest, which is, in turn determined using annuity tables issued by the IRS. If the trust assets grow at a rate that exceeds the statutory interest rate assumed in the annuity tables, the excess appreciation ultimately will be transferred to the remainder beneficiaries, free of transfer tax. If, however, the grantor dies during the trust term, the portion of the trust assets necessary to satisfy the annuity are included in the grantor's estate for estate tax purposes.

The GRAT structure allows taxpayers to fund GRATs aggressively, with little downside risk. In some cases, for example, taxpayers "zero out" a GRAT by structuring the trust so that the value of the annuity interest equals (or nearly equals) the entire value of the property transferred to the trust. Under this strategy, the value of the remainder interest - and hence the value of any gift that is subject to gift taxation - is deemed to be equal to or near zero. In reality, however, by funding GRATs with assets expected to significantly increase in value, taxpayers often achieve returns on trust assets substantially in excess of the returns assumed under the annuity tables, which allows any excess appreciation to pass to heirs without transfer taxation. Furthermore, grantors often structure GRATs with relatively short terms, such as two years, to minimize the risk that the grantor will die during the trust term, causing the assets to be included in the grantor's estate. Taxpayers sometimes establish multiple, concurrent GRATs funded with different assets in an effort to increase the likelihood that at least one will succeed during any given period.

In its Fiscal Year 2016 budget, the Administration proposes to modify the tax rules for GRATs to require that the GRAT have a term of at least 10 years and that the remainder have a value equal to the greater of 25 percent of the value of assets contributed to the GRAT or $500,000 (but no more than the amount contributed).[130] Similar proposals have been included in several introduced bills.[131] The proposal generally seeks to introduce down-side risk into GRATs, minimizing or eliminating taxpayers' ability aggressively to fund GRATs in an effort to outperform annuity assumptions with little risk of loss.

Limit the Generation-Skipping Transfer Tax Exemption for Dynasty Trusts

Another proposal seeks to limit taxpayers' ability to establish trusts that will exist in perpetuity and that will forever be exempt from the generation-skipping transfer tax. In general, where a taxpayer allocates generation-skipping transfer tax exemption to a trust in an amount equal to assets transferred to the trust, all future distributions from or terminations of interests in that trust will be exempt from generation-skipping transfer tax, no matter when they occur. Historically, this ability to create perpetually exempt trusts was mitigated by State law "rules against perpetuities" that limit the legal lifespan of a trust. In recent years, however, many States have repealed their rules against perpetuities, with the effect that taxpayers now can establish exempt trusts that will exist in perpetuity and which can grow quite large, allowing vast sums to be passed to future generations without transfer tax consequences. These trusts sometimes are referred to as dynasty trusts.

In its Fiscal Year 2016 budget, the Administration proposes to modify the transfer tax laws to provide that, on the 90th anniversary of the creation of a trust, any generation-skipping transfer tax exemption allocated to the trust would terminate.[132] Taxpayers thus could continue to create trusts that are exempt from generation-skipping transfer tax for a period of time, but the exemption could not exist in perpetuity. Similar proposals have been included in introduced bills.[133]

Require Consistency in Value for Transfer and Income Tax Purposes

A third proposal would coordinate the valuation rules for transfer and income tax purposes. The value of an asset for purposes of the estate tax generally is the fair market value at the time of death or at the alternate valuation date. The basis of property acquired from a decedent is the fair market value of the property at the time of the decedent's death or as of an alternate valuation date, if elected by the executor. Under regulations, the fair market value of the property at the date of the decedent's death (or alternate valuation date) is deemed to be its value as appraised for estate tax purposes.[134] However, the value of property as reported on the decedent's estate tax return provides only a rebuttable presumption of the property's basis in the hands of the heir.[135] Unless the heir is estopped by his or her previous actions or statements with regard to the estate tax valuation, the heir may rebut the use of the estate's valuation as his or her basis by clear and convincing evidence.[136]

Generally the incentive exists for an executor of an estate or a donor of a lifetime gift to offer low estimates of the value of assets for estate or gift tax purposes in order to minimize the amount of transfer tax. For the purpose of determining gain or loss on an inherited asset or on an asset received by gift, however, generally the recipient would prefer a higher basis.[137] The government is potentially whipsawed by inconsistent valuations.

The proposal seeks to address this concern by requiring that the recipient's basis of property equal the value used by the transferor for transfer tax purposes. The Administration included a version of this proposal in its Fiscal Year 2016 budget, requiring consistency both in the case of gifts and transfers at death. [138] The "Tax Relief Act of 2014," introduced by Congressman Dave Camp, included a similar proposal, but limited its application to transfers at death.[139]

E. Proposal to Tax Built-in Gains at the Time of a Gift or upon Death

A proposal included in the Administration's Fiscal Year 2016 budget would require the recognition of any built-in gain at the time of a gift or upon death.[140] Under present law, capital gains generally are taxable only when an appreciated asset is sold or otherwise disposed of. A gift or bequest generally is not treated as a sale or disposition; therefore, there is no realization of built-in gain upon the gift or bequest of an appreciated asset. The recipient of a gift generally takes the donor's basis in the assets transferred, such that the recipient generally recognizes gain on the appreciation at the time of a subsequent sale or disposition. A taxpayer who receives assets from a decedent, however, generally receives a basis equal to the fair market value of the asset as of the decedent's death. As a result, any appreciation that occurred during the decedent's life is never subjected to income tax.

The Administration's proposal generally treats transfers of appreciated property by gift or at death as a sale of the property. As a result, the transferor (the donor of a gift or the deceased owner of an asset), would realize capital gain at the time of the transfer equal to the excess of the asset's fair market value over the transferor's basis in the asset. In the case of a decedent, the capital gain generally would be included on a final income tax return.

The proposal contains a number of special rules. First, gifts or bequests to a spouse would take the basis of the transferor, and no gain would be realized until the receiving spouse sells or disposes of the asset. The proposal exempts from capital gains tax transfers to charity and transfers of tangible personal property, such as household furnishings and personal effects. Each taxpayer also would be allowed an exclusion of $100,000 ($200,000 per married couple) of gain recognized upon gift or at death, with any unused amount portable to the surviving spouse. In addition, the present-law $250,000 per person exclusion for capital gain on a personal residence would apply to all residences, and any unused exclusion would be portable to a surviving spouse.

The present-law exclusion for capital gain on certain small business stock would apply. In addition, any appreciation of certain small family-owned and family-operated businesses would be deferred and recognized only when the business is sold by the recipient or ceases to be family-owned and operated. The proposal allows a 15-year fixed-rate payment plan for the tax on appreciated assets transferred at death, other than liquid assets (such as publicly traded stock) or businesses for which the deferral election is made.

The Administration argues that the proposal is necessary, because present-law capital gain rules unfairly favor wealthier taxpayers relative to less wealthy taxpayers.[141] Specifically, the Administration states that when an individual has more resources than he or she needs during retirement such that the individual is able to leave appreciated assets to heirs, any built-in gain permanently escapes taxation. A less wealthy individual, on the other hand, often must spend down his or her assets during retirement and must pay tax on any realized gains.

Furthermore, the Administration argues that the preferential treatment for assets held until death produces an inefficient lock-in effect on capital, *i.e.*, taxpayers hold assets solely to avoid paying tax on gains, rather than more productively reinvesting capital. Opponents of the proposal might argue that a tax on built-in gain when assets are transferred by gift or at death, particularly when combined with the present-law wealth transfer taxes, will burden taxpayers, particularly owners of small businesses and family farms.

End Notes

[1] This document may be cited as follows: Joint Committee on Taxation, *History, Present Law, and Analysis of the Federal Wealth Transfer Tax System* (JCX-52-15), March 16, 2015.

[2] Darien B. Jacobson, Brian G. Raub, and Barry W. Johnson, "The Estate Tax: Ninety Years and Counting," in Internal Revenue Service, *Statistics of Income Bulletin* (Summer 2007), p. 125.

[3] Sec. 2010. Except as otherwise noted, all section references are to the Internal Revenue Code of 1986, as amended (the "Code").

[4] The generation-skipping transfer tax exemption is equal to the applicable exemption in effect for estate tax purposes in any given year.

[5] Pub. L. No. 107-16, Title V (June 7, 2001).

[6] See the Tax Relief, Unemployment Insurance Reauthorization, and Job Creation Act of 2010, Pub. L. No. 111-312 (Dec. 17, 2010).

[7] See the American Taxpayer Relief Act of 2012, Pub. L. No. 112-240 (Jan. 2, 2013).

[8] Act of July 6, 1797, 1 Stat. 527.

[9] Act of June 30, 1802, 2 Stat. 148.

[10] Inheritance taxes typically are imposed on the recipient of a transfer from a decedent, whereas estate taxes are imposed on a decedent's estate.

[11] Act of July 1, 1862, 12 Stat. 432, 483; Act of July 15, 1870, 16 Stat. 256.

[12] War Revenue Act of 1898, 30 Stat. 448, 464 (July 4, 1898).

[13] Act of April 12, 1902, 32 Stat. 96.

[14] See quotation in Randolph E. Paul, *Taxation in the United States*, p. 88 (Boston 1954).

[15] Act of September 8, 1916, 39 Stat. 756.

[16] The present-law rule is now contained in section 2043.

[17] The present-law rule is now contained in section 2037.

[18] Act of March 3, 1917, 39 Stat. 1000.

[19] The present-law rules are now contained in sections 2041 and 2514.

[20] The present-law rule is now contained in section 2038.

[21] Revenue Act of 1932, 47 Stat. 169 (June 6, 1932).

[22] The present-law rule is now contained in section 2036(a).

[23] Act of May 10, 1934, 48 Stat. 680.

[24] Act of August 30, 1935, 49 Stat. 1014.

[25] Revenue Act of 1940, 54 Stat. 516.

[26] Act of September 20, 1941, 55 Stat. 687.

[27] The $60,000 death-time and the $30,000 lifetime exemptions remained at these levels until the Tax Reform Act of 1976, when the estate and gift taxes were combined into a single unified tax that could be reduced by a unified credit which replaced the two exemptions.

[28] Act of October 21, 1942, 56 Stat. 798.

[29] Revenue Act of 1948, 62 Stat. 110.

[30] The present-law rule is now contained in section 2042.

[31] Pub. L. No. 85-866 (Sept. 2, 1958).

[32] The present-law rule has been subsequently modified; it is now contained in section 6166.

[33] Pub. L. No. 94-455 (Oct. 4, 1976).

[34] The present-law rules are now contained in sections 2001 and 2501.

[35] The present-law "special-use valuation" rules are contained in section 2032A, and require heirs to continue to use the property for only 10 years after the decedent's death. The 1976 Act also: (1) changed the treatment of gifts made in contemplation of death from a rebuttable presumption that gifts made within three years of death would be subject to estate tax to a rule that subjects certain gifts made within three years of death to the estate tax; (2) provided that each spouse was rebuttably presumed to have contributed equally to the acquisition cost of jointly-held property; (3) provided a limited deduction for bequests to children with no living parents (the so-called "orphan's deduction"); and (4) provided statutory rules governing the disclaimer of gifts and bequests under which an unqualified, irrevocable refusal to accept any benefits from the gift or bequest generally within 9 months of the creation of the transferee's interest is not treated as a gift by the disclaiming individual.

[36] Crude Oil Windfall Profits Act of 1980, Pub. L. No. 96-223 (Apr. 2, 1980).

[37] Pub. L. No. 97-34 (Aug. 13, 1981).

[38] The present-law rule is now contained in section 2056. The 1981 Act also: (1) increased the annual gift tax exemption from $3,000 per year per donee to $10,000 per year per donee; (2) changed the presumption that each spouse equally provided for the acquisition cost of jointly-held property to an irrebuttable presumption; (3) repealed the so-called "orphan's deduction"; and (4) delayed the effective date of the generation-skipping transfer tax.

[39] Pub. L. No. 98-369 (July 18, 1984). For example, the 1984 Act: (1) delayed for three years the scheduled reduction of the maximum estate and gift tax rates (such that the maximum rate remained at 55 percent until 1988); (2) eliminated the exclusion for interests in qualified retirement plans; (3) provided rules for the gift and income tax treatment of below-market rate loans; and (4) extended the rules that permit the installment payment of estate taxes on closely held businesses to certain holding companies.

[40] Pub. L. No. 99-514 (Oct. 22, 1986). The present-law generation-skipping transfer tax rules added by the Tax Reform Act of 1986 are contained in sections 2601 through 2654.

[41] Pub. L. No. 100-203 (Dec. 22, 1987).

[42] Pub. L. No. 101-508 (Nov. 5, 2990).

[43] The present-law rules are contained in sections 2701 through 2704.

[44] Pub. L. No. 103-66 (Aug. 10, 1993).

[45] Pub. L. No. 105-34 (Aug. 5, 1997).

[46] Pub. L. No. 107-16 (June 7, 2001).

[47] Sec. 102.

[48] Sec. 2010.

[49] For 2011 and later years, the gift and estate taxes were reunified, meaning that the gift tax exemption amount was increased to equal the estate tax exemption amount.

[50] For 2015, the $5.43 exemption amount results in a unified credit of $2,117,800, after applying the applicable rates set forth in section 2001(c).

[51] Secs. 2056 and 2523.

[52] Secs. 2055 and 2522.

[53] Sec. 2055(d).

[54] Secs. 2055(e)(2) and 2522(c)(2).

[55] Sec. 2001(a).

[56] More mechanically, the taxable estate is combined with the value of adjusted taxable gifts made during the decedent's life (generally, post-1976 gifts), before applying tax rates to

determine a tentative total amount of tax. The portion of the tentative tax attributable to lifetime gifts is then subtracted from the total tentative tax to determine the gross estate tax, *i.e.*, the amount of estate tax before considering available credits. Credits are then subtracted to determine the estate tax liability.

This method of computation was designed to ensure that a taxpayer only gets one run up through the rate brackets for all lifetime gifts and transfers at death, at a time when the thresholds for applying the higher marginal rates exceeded the exemption amount. However, the higher ($5.43 million) present-law exemption amount effectively renders the lower rate brackets irrelevant, because the top marginal rate bracket applies to all transfers in excess of $1 million. In other words, all transfers that are not exempt by reason of the $5.43 million exemption amount are taxed at the highest marginal rate of 40 percent.

[57] Sec. 2031(a).

[58] Sec. 2032.

[59] Sec. 2033.

[60] Sec. 2035.

[61] Sec. 2036.

[62] Sec. 2037.

[63] Sec. 2038.

[64] Sec. 2041.

[65] Sec. 2042.

[66] Sec. 2058.

[67] Sec. 2053.

[68] Sec. 2054.

[69] Sec. 2010.

[70] Sec. 2012.

[71] Sec. 2013.

[72] Sec. 2014. In certain cases, an election may be made to deduct foreign death taxes. See section 2053(d).

[73] Sec. 2032A.

[74] Prior to 2004, an estate also was permitted to deduct the adjusted value of a qualified family-owned business interest of the decedent, up to $675,000. Sec. 2057. A qualified family-owned business interest generally was defined as any interest in a trade or business (regardless of the form in which it is held) with a principal place of business in the United States if the decedent's family owns at least 50 percent of the trade or business, two families own 70 percent, or three families own 90 percent, as long as the decedent's family owns at least 30 percent of the trade or business. To qualify for the exclusion, the decedent (or a member of the decedent's family) must have owned and materially participated in the trade or business for at least five of the eight years preceding the decedent's date of death. In addition, at least one qualified heir (or member of the qualified heir's family) was required to have materially participated in the trade or business for at least 10 years following the decedent's death. The qualified family-owned business rules provided a graduated recapture based on the number of years after the decedent's death within which a disqualifying event occurred.

The qualified family-owned business deduction and the unified credit effective exemption amount were coordinated. If the maximum deduction amount of $675,000 is elected, then the unified credit effective exemption amount is $625,000, for a total of $1.3 million. If the qualified family-owned business deduction is less than $675,000, then the unified credit effective exemption amount is equal to $625,000, increased by the difference between

$675,000 and the amount of the qualified family-owned business deduction. However, the unified credit effective exemption amount cannot be increased above such amount in effect for the taxable year. Because of the coordination between the qualified family-owned business deduction and the unified credit effective exemption amount, the qualified family-owned business deduction did not provide a benefit in any year in which the applicable exclusion amount exceeded $1.3 million.

[75] Sec. 6166.

[76] The interest rate on this portion adjusts with the Federal short-term rate.

[77] Sec. 2501(a).

[78] Sec. 2511(a).

[79] Sec. 2512(a).

[80] Sec. 2512(b).

[81] Sec. 2503(e).

[82] Sec. 2501(a)(4).

[83] Sec. 2503(b).

[84] Sec. 529(c)(2).

[85] The inclusion ratio is one minus the applicable fraction. The applicable fraction is the amount of exemption allocated to a trust (or to a direct skip) divided by the value of assets transferred.

[86] The 1988 percentage of decedents liable for estate tax of 0.87 may overstate the nadir achieved by the increase in the unified credit to an exemption equivalent amount of $600,000. This is because the 1981 legislation also increased the marital exemption to an unlimited exemption. An increase in the marital exemption would be expected to reduce the percentage of decedents liable for the estate tax, both permanently and during a temporary period following the increase. The permanent effect results from some married couples having neither spouse liable for estate tax. The temporary reduction in the percentage of decedents liable for estate tax arises as follows. A married couple may have sufficient assets to be subject to the estate tax. During the transition period in which husbands and wives first take advantage of the unlimited marital exemption, the number of decedents liable for estate tax falls as the first spouse to die takes advantage of the expanded marital deduction, despite the fact that the surviving spouse subsequently dies with a taxable estate. In the long run, the number of new couples utilizing the unlimited marital deduction may be expected to approximately equal the number of surviving spouses becoming taxable after their decedent spouse had claimed the unlimited marital deduction.

[87] The analysis of the text assumes that the capital accumulated is physical or business intangible capital. Real per capita GNP could grow if individuals accumulated more knowledge and skills, or what economists call "human capital." Accumulation of human capital unaccompanied by the accumulation of physical or business intangible capital would not necessarily lead to increasing numbers of decedents becoming liable for estate tax.

[88] This analysis assumes that the capital accumulation is held broadly. If the growth in the capital stock were all due to a declining number of individuals doing the accumulating, then the distribution of wealth would become less equal and real growth could be accompanied by a declining percentage of decedents being liable for estate tax. Alternatively, if all of the capital accumulation accrued to individuals far below the exemption threshold, then even though the distribution of wealth becomes more equal, real growth could also be accompanied by a declining percentage of decedents being liable for estate tax.

[89] See David Joulfaian, "The Federal Estate and Gift Tax: Description, Profile of Taxpayers, and Economic Consequences," *U.S. Department of the Treasury*, OTA Paper 80, December

1998. Table 19 of that publication displays the life expectancy of a surviving spouse and shows that 55 percent of spouses die within 10 years of the first-to-die spouse.

[90] The 2010 Act provided that in the case of a decedent dying during 2010, the executor could elect to apply the law as originally enacted under EGTRRA (*i.e.*, repeal of the estate tax and the application of the modified carryover basis rules for assets acquired from a decedent).

[91] Economists call income and consumption "flow" concepts. In simple terms, a flow can only be measured by reference to a unit of time. Thus, one refers to a taxpayer's annual income or monthly consumption expenditures.

[92] Economists call wealth a "stock" concept. A stock of wealth, such as a bank account, may generate a flow of income, such as annual interest income.

[93] James Poterba, "The Estate Tax and After-Tax Investment Returns," in Joel B. Slemrod, ed., *Does Atlas Shrug? The Economic Consequences of Taxing the Rich* (New York and Cambridge: Russell Sage Foundation and Harvard University Press), 2000. Poterba converts the estate tax to a tax on capital income with the effective tax rate depending on the statutory tax rate as well as the potential taxpayer's mortality risk.

[94] For a discussion of economic incidence of capital taxes in the context of taxes on business income, see Joint Committee on Taxation, *Modeling the Distribution of Taxes on Business Income* (JCX-14-13), October 16, 2013.

[95] See B. Douglas Bernheim, "Taxation and Saving" in Alan J. Auerbach and Martin Feldstein (eds.), *Handbook of Public Economics*, vol. 3, Elsevier Science Publishers, 2002, pp. 1173-1249, and Douglas W. Elmendorf, "The Effect of Interest-Rate Changes on Household Saving and Consumption: a Survey," *Finance and Economics Discussion Series*, 96-27, (Board of Governors of the Federal Reserve System), 1996.

[96] A discussion of why, theoretically, the effect of the estate tax on saving behavior depends upon taxpayers' motives for intergenerational transfers and wealth accumulation is provided by William G. Gale and Maria G. Perozek, "Do Estate Taxes Reduce Saving?" in William G. Gale and Joel B. Slemrod (eds.), *Rethinking the Estate Tax*, The Brookings Institution, 2001. For a brief review of how different views of the bequest motive may alter taxpayer bequest behavior, see William G. Gale and Joel B. Slemrod, "Death Watch for the Estate Tax," *Journal of Economic Perspectives*, vol. 15, Winter 2001, pp. 205-218.

[97] See Laurence J. Kotlikoff and Lawrence H. Summers, "The Role of Intergenerational Transfers in Aggregate Capital Accumulation," *Journal of Political Economy*, vol. 89, August 1981. Also see, Laurence J. Kotlikoff, "Intergenerational Transfers and Savings," *Journal of Economic Perspectives*, vol. 2, Spring 1988. For discussion of these issues in the context of wealth transfer taxes see, Henry J. Aaron and Alicia H. Munnell, "Reassessing the Role for Wealth Transfer Taxes," *National Tax Journal*, vol. 45, June 1992. For attempts to calculate the share of the aggregate capital stock attributable to the bequest motive, see Thomas A. Barthold and Takatoshi Ito, "Bequest Taxes and Accumulation of Household Wealth: U.S.-Japan Comparison," in Takatoshi Ito and Anne O. Kreuger (eds.), *The Political Economy of Tax Reform*, The University of Chicago Press, 1992; and William G. Gale and John Karl Scholz, "Intergenerational Transfers and the Accumulation of Wealth," *Journal of Economic Perspectives*, vol. 8, Fall 1994, pp. 145-160. Gale and Scholz estimate that 20 percent of the nation's capital stock can be attributed to "intentional transfers" (including *inter vivos* transfers, life insurance, and trusts) and another 30 percent can be attributed to bequests, whether planned or unplanned.

[98] Franco Modigliani, "The Role of Intergenerational Transfers and Life Cycle Saving in the Accumulation of Wealth," *Journal of Economic Perspectives*, vol. 2, Spring 1988. In this article, Modigliani argues that 15 percent is more likely an upper bound.

[99] See B. Douglas Bernheim, "How Strong Are Bequest Motives? Evidence Based on Estimates of the Demand for Life Insurance and Annuities," *Journal of Political Economy*, vol. 99, October 1991, pp. 899-927. Bernheim finds that social security annuity benefits raise life insurance holdings and depress private annuity holdings among elderly individuals. He interprets this as evidence that elderly individuals choose to maintain a positive fraction of their resources in bequeathable forms. For an opposing finding, see Michael D. Hurd, "Savings of the Elderly and Desired Bequests," *American Economic Review*, vol. 77, June 1987, pp. 298-312. Hurd concludes that "any bequest motive is not an important determinant of consumption decisions and wealth holdings.... Bequests seem to be simply the result of mortality risk combined with a very weak market for private annuities." *Ibid.*, p. 308.

[100] Wojciech Kopczuk and Joel Slemrod, "The Impact of the Estate Tax on the Wealth Accumulation and Avoidance Behavior of Donors," in William G. Gale and Joel B. Slemrod (eds.), *Rethinking Estate and Gift Taxation*, The Brookings Institution, 2001, use estate tax return data from 1916 to 1996 to investigate the impact of the estate tax on reported estates. They find a negative correlation between measures of the level of estate taxation and reported wealth. This finding may be consistent with the estate tax depressing wealth accumulation (depressing saving) or with the estate tax encouraging successful avoidance activity.

More recently, David Joulfaian, "The Behavioral Response of Wealth Accumulation to Estate Taxation: Time Series Evidence," *National Tax Journal*, vol. 59, June 2006, pp. 253-268, examines the size of taxable estates and the structure of the estate tax and its effects on the expected rates of return to saving. While he emphasizes the sensitivity of the analysis to how individuals' expectations about future taxes are modeled he concludes that "taxable estates are ten percent smaller because of the estate tax."

[101] Andrew Carnegie, "The Advantages of Poverty," in *The Gospel of Wealth and Other Timely Essays,* Edward C. Kirkland (ed.), The Belknap Press of Harvard University Press, 1962, reprint of Carnegie from 1891.

[102] For a review of this issue, see John Pencavel, "Labor Supply of Men: A Survey," in Orley Ashenfelter and Richard Layard (eds.), *Handbook of Labor Economics*, vol. I, North-Holland Publishing Co., 1986. For a direct empirical test of what some refer to as the "Carnegie Conjecture," see Douglas Holtz-Eakin, David Joulfaian, and Harvey S. Rosen, "The Carnegie Conjecture: Some Empirical Evidence," *Quarterly Journal of Economics*, vol. 108, May 1993, pp. 413-435. Holtz-Eakin, Joulfaian, and Rosen assess the labor force participation of families that receive an inheritance. They find that "the likelihood that a person decreases his or her participation in the labor force increases with the size of the inheritance received. For example, families with one or two earners who received inheritances above $150,000 [in 1982-1985 constant dollars] were about three times more likely to reduce their labor force participation to zero than families with inheritances below $25,000. Moreover, ... high inheritance families experienced lower earnings growth than low inheritance families, which is consistent with the notion that inheritance reduces hours of work." *Ibid.*, pp. 432-433. Theory suggests also that those who choose to remain in the labor force will reduce their hours worked or labor earnings. Holtz-Eakin, Joulfaian, and Rosen find these effects to be small.

[103] For some exceptions, see Martin H. David and Paul L. Menchik, "Changes in Cohort Wealth Over a Generation," *Demography*, vol. 25, August 1988; Paul L. Menchik and Martin H. David, "The Effect of Income Distribution on Lifetime Savings and Bequests," *American Economic Review*, vol. 73, September 1983; and Edward N. Wolff, "Estimate of Household

Wealth Inequality in the U.S., 1962-1983," *The Review of Income and Wealth*, vol. 33, September 1987.

[104] See, for example, Thomas Piketty and Gabriel Zucman, "Capital is Back: Wealth-Income Ratios in Rich Countries 1700-2010," *Quarterly Journal of Economics*, vol. 129, no. 3, August 2014, pp. 1255-1310, and Alan J. Auerbach and Kevin Hassett, "Capital Taxation in the 21st Century," National Bureau of Economic Research Working Paper No. 20871, January 2015.

[105] See Michael K. Taussig, "Les inégalités de patrimoine aux Etats-Unis," in Kessler, Masson, Strauss-Khan (eds.), *Accumulation et Repartition des Patrimoines*. Taussig estimates shares of wealth held by the top 0.5 percent of wealth holders in the United States for various years between 1922 and 1972. Wolff, in "Estimate of Household Wealth Inequality in the U.S., 1962-1983," does not attribute any movements in wealth distribution directly to tax policy, but rather to the changes in the relative values of housing and corporate stock.

Wojciech Kopczuk and Joel Slemrod, "The Impact of the Estate Tax on Wealth Accumulation and Avoidance Behavior," in William G. Gale, James R. Hines Jr., and Joel Slemrod (eds.), *Rethinking Estate and Gift Taxation* (The Brookings Institution) 2001, find mixed evidence. Using aggregate time series data, Kopczuk and Slemrod find a negative correlation between the share of wealth held by top wealth holders and the estate tax rates.

That finding would imply that the estate tax may mitigate the concentration of wealth among top wealth holders. Wojciech Kopczuk and Emmanuel Saez, "Top Wealth Shares in the United States, 1916-2000: Evidence from Estate Tax Returns," *National Tax Journal*, vol. 57, September 2004, pp. 445-487, report a similar result. However, when Kopczuk and Slemrod use pooled cross section analysis to make use of individual estate tax return data, they find at best a weak relationship between estate tax rates and wealth holdings.

[106] Based on the 1998 Survey of Consumer Finance, one study estimates expected unrealized capital gains at death represent 36 percent of total expected value of estates. For estates worth at least $10 million, unrealized capital gains at death represent 56 percent of the value of estates. For this group of estates, the largest component (72.3 percent) of unrealized gains is estimated to be attributable to unrealized capital gains on active businesses of decedents. James Poterba and Scott Weisbenner, "The Distributional Burden of Taxing Estates and Unrealized Capital Gains at Death," in William G. Gale, James R. Hines, Jr., and Joel Slemrod (eds.), *Rethinking Estate and Gift Taxation* (Brookings Institution Press) 2001, pp. 422-449. In addition to the unrealized capital gains considered here, the value of other assets included in the value of an estate may have previously received favorable income tax treatment. For example, the Survey of Consumer Finance does not collect information on unrealized gains in retirement accounts. Brian K. Bucks, Arthur B. Kennickell, Traci L. Mach, and Kevin B. Moore, "Changes in U.S. Family Finances from 2004 to 2007: Evidence from the Survey of Consumer Finances," *Federal Reserve Bulletin*, vol. 95, February 2009, p. A36-A37.

[107] Researchers have found that the correlation of income between parents and children is less than perfect. For analysis of the correlation of income among family members across generations, see Gary R. Solon, "Intergenerational Income Mobility in the United States," *American Economic Review*, vol. 82, June 1992, and David J. Zimmerman, "Regression Toward Mediocrity in Economic Stature," *American Economic Review*, vol. 82, June 1992. These studies, however, examine data relating to a broad range of incomes in the United States and do not directly assess the correlation of income among family members with transferors subject to the estate tax.

[108] Economists note that when expenditures on specified items are permitted to be deducted from the tax base, before the computation of tax liability, the price of the deductible item is effectively reduced by a percentage equal to the taxpayer's marginal tax rate. Assume, for example, a decedent has a $1 million taxable estate and that the marginal, and average, estate tax rate was 40 percent. This means that the estate tax liability would be $400,000. A net of $600,000 would be available for distribution to heirs. If, however, the decedent had provided that his estate make a charitable bequest of $100,000, the taxable estate would equal $900,000 and the estate tax liability would be $360,000. By bequeathing $100,000 to charity, the estate's tax liability fell by $40,000. The net available for distribution to heirs after payment of the estate tax and payment of the charitable bequest would be $540,000. The $100,000 charitable bequest reduced the amount of funds available to be distributed to heirs by only $60,000. Economists say that the $100,000 charitable bequest "cost" $60,000, or that the "price" of the bequest was 60 cents per dollar of bequest. More generally, the "price" of charitable bequest equals (1 - t), where t is the estate's marginal tax rate.

[109] For example, see Charles T. Clotfelter, *Federal Tax Policy and Charitable Giving*, University of Chicago Press, 1985; David Joulfaian, "Charitable Bequests and Estate Taxes," *National Tax Journal*, vol. 44, June 1991, pp. 169-180; and Gerald Auten and David Joulfaian, "Charitable Contributions and Intergenerational Transfers," *Journal of Public Economics*, vol. 59, 1996, pp. 55-68. David Joulfaian, "Estate Taxes and Charitable Bequests by the Wealthy," *National Tax Journal*, vol. 53, September 2000, pp. 743-763, provides a survey of these studies and presents new evidence. Each of these studies estimates a tax price elasticity in excess of 1.6 in absolute value. This implies that for each 10-percent reduction in the tax price, where the tax price is defined as one minus the marginal tax rate, there is a greater than 16-percent increase in the dollar value of charitable bequests. Such a finding implies that charities receive a greater dollar value of bequests than the Treasury loses in forgone tax revenue. In a more recent study, Michael J. Brunetti, "The Estate Tax and Charitable Bequests: Elasticity Estimates Using Probate Records," *National Tax Journal*, vol. 58, June 2005, pp. 165-188, finds price elasticities in excess of 1.2.

Not all studies find such responsiveness of charitable bequests to the marginal estate tax rate. Thomas Barthold and Robert Plotnick, "Estate Taxation and Other Determinants of Charitable Bequests," *National Tax Journal*, vol. 37, June 1984, pp. 225-237, estimated that marginal tax rates had no effect on charitable bequests.

[110] Auten and Joulfaian, "Charitable Contributions and Intergenerational Transfers," attempted to estimate this more complex framework. Their findings suggest that reductions in estate taxation would reduce charitable contributions during the taxpayer's life.

[111] Joint Economic Committee, *The Economics of the Estate Tax*, December 1998, has stated "the costs of complying with the estate tax laws are roughly the same magnitude as the revenue raised." Richard Schmalbeck, "Avoiding Federal Wealth Transfer Taxes," in William G. Gale and Joel B. Slemrod (eds.), *Rethinking Estate and Gift Taxation* (The Brookings Institution) 2001, disagrees writing "[a]bout half of the estate planners consulted in the preparation of this paper reported that they had rather standard packages that they would make available to individuals who would leave estates in the three to ten million range that might be provided for as little as $3000 to $5000." See William G. Gale and Joel B. Slemrod, "Life and Death Questions About the Estate and Gift Tax," *National Tax Journal*, vol. 53, December 2000, pp. 889-912, for a review of the literature on compliance cost.

[112] Eight states have some form of Inheritance Tax. See McGuire Woods LLP State Death Tax Chart, Revised March 26, 2012, available at http://www.mcguirewoods.com/news-resources/publications/taxation/state_death_tax_chart.pdf .

[113] See, *e.g.*, Lily L. Batchelder, "Taxing Privilege More Effectively: Replacing the Estate Tax with an Inheritance Tax," The Hamilton Project, The Brookings Institution, Discussion Paper 2007-07, June 2007, p. 5; "Alternatives to the Current Wealth Transfer Tax System," in American Bar Association, Task Force on Federal Wealth Transfer Taxes, "Report on Reform of Federal Wealth Transfer Taxes," 2004, p. 171, app. A.; Joseph M. Dodge, "Comparing a Reformed Estate Tax with an Accessions Tax and an Income-Inclusion System, and Abandoning the Generation-Skipping Tax," *SMU Law Review*, vol. 56, 2003, pp. 551, 556.

[114] Steven M. Fazzari, R. Glenn Hubbard, and Bruce C. Petersen, "Financing Constraints and Corporate Investment," *Brookings Papers on Economic Activity*, 1988, pp. 141-195.

[115] Douglas Holtz-Eakin, David Joulfaian, and Harvey S. Rosen, "Sticking It Out: Entrepreneurial Survival and Liquidity Constraints," *Journal of Political Economy*, vol. 102, February 1994, pp. 53-75. Holtz-Eakin, Joulfaian, and Rosen study the effect of receipt of an inheritance on whether an entrepreneur's business survives rather than whether an on-going business that is taxed as an asset in an individual's estate survives. They find that "the effect of inheritance on the probability of surviving as an entrepreneur is small but noticeable: a $150,000 inheritance raises the probability of survival by about 1.3 percentage points," and "[i]f enterprises do survive, inheritances have a substantial impact on their performance: the $150,000 inheritance ... is associated with a nearly 20-percent increase in an enterprise's receipts." *Ibid.*, p.74.

These results do not necessarily imply that the aggregate economy is made better off by receipt of inheritances. Survival of the entrepreneur may not be the most highly valued investment that could be made with the funds received. For example, Francisco Perez-Gonzalez, "Inherited Control and Firm Performance," *American Economic Review*, vol. 96, December 2006, pp. 1559-1589, finds that where the incoming CEO is related to the departing CEO, or to a founder, the firm underperforms in terms of profitability and other financial measures.

[116] See George Cooper, *A Voluntary Tax? New Perspectives on Sophisticated Tax Avoidance* (The Brookings Institution) 1979. Also, see B. Douglas Bernheim, "Does the Estate Tax Raise Revenue?" in Lawrence H. Summers (ed.), *Tax Policy and the Economy* 1 (The MIT Press) 1987; and Alicia H. Munnell with Nicole Ernsberger, "Wealth Transfer Taxation: The Relative Role for Estate and Income Taxes," *New England Economic Review*, November/December 1988. These studies pre-date the enactment of chapter 14 of the Code. The purpose of chapter 14 is to improve reporting of asset values in certain transfers. Nevertheless, planning opportunities remain whereby small business owners can reduce the cash required to meet an estate tax obligation, see Joint Committee on Taxation, *Options to Improve Tax Compliance and Reform Tax Expenditures* (JCS-2-05), January 27, 2005. The Joint Committee staff discusses the ability to use valuation discounts and lapsing trust powers effectively to shelter business (and other) assets from the estate tax on pages 396-408.

[117] Martha Eller Gangi and Brian G. Raub, "Utilization of Special Estate Tax Provisions for Family-Owned Farms and Closely Held Businesses," *SOI Bulletin*, 26, Summer 2006, pp. 128-145. Gangi and Raub report that in 2001 of 12,683 estates with farm real estate, 831 elected special use valuation; of 15,612 estates with closely held businesses or agri-business assets, 1,144 claimed a deduction for qualified family-owned business interests; and 382 estates elected to defer payment of the estate tax.

[118] *Ibid.*, Figures D and I.

[119] *Ibid.*, Figure N.

[120] *Ibid.*, Figures D, I, and N.

[121] On the other hand, when resources are used to purchase insurance, those resources are no longer available for investment opportunities.

[122] This is not conceptually correct as mathematically if an estate has any liquid assets and no tax or debt liability the liquidity ratio would be infinite. An infinite value would render reported averages as meaningless. However, it is important to recognize that an estate could also have liquidity ratio of zero if it had no liquid assets and some, however modest, estate tax or debt liability. In the 2011 data almost all of the zero liquidity ratios are estates with no estate tax liabilities.

[123] The continuing operation of the farm could be impaired by a reduction in liquid operating capital.

[124] This is similar to Table 7 in JCX-108-07, but reports data from estate tax returns filed in a more recent year. The 2003 included information on estates that claimed benefits under section 2057. The special deduction available under section 2057 was not available for estates in 2013.

[125] This is similar to Table 8 in JCX-108-07, but reports data from estate tax returns filed in a more recent year. The 2003 table included information on estates that claimed benefits under section 2057. The special deduction available under section 2057 was not available for estates in 2013.

[126] H.R. 1105 (114th Cong., 1st Sess.).

[127] A separate bill introduced by Congressman Tim Griffin, also titled the "Death Tax Repeal Act," would repeal not only the estate and generation-skipping transfer taxes, but also the gift tax. H.R. 177 (113th Cong., 2d Sess.).

[128] Department of the Treasury, *General Explanations of the Administration's Fiscal Year 2016 Revenue Proposals,* February 2015, pp. 193-94.

[129] H.R. 4061 (113th Cong. 2d Sess.).

[130] Department of the Treasury, *General Explanations of the Administration's Fiscal Year 2016 Revenue Proposals,* February 2015, pp. 197-99.

[131] See, *e.g.*, sec. 6 of the "Sensible Estate Tax Act of 2014." H.R. 4061 (113th Cong. 2d Sess.). A similar provision passed the U.S. House of Representatives three times in 2010. See sec. 307 of H.R. 4849 (111sth Cong., 2d Sess.), passed by the U.S. House of Representatives on March 25, 2010; sec. 531 of H.R. 5486 (111sth Cong., 2d Sess.), passed by the U.S. House of Representatives on June 15, 2010; and H.R. 4899 (111sth Cong., 2d Sess.), passed by the U.S. House of Representatives on July 1, 2010.

[132] Department of the Treasury, *General Explanations of the Administration's Fiscal Year 2016 Revenue Proposals,* February 2015, pp. 200-01.

[133] See, *e.g.*, sec. 7 of the "Sensible Estate Tax Act of 2014." H.R. 4061 (113th Cong. 2d Sess.). For a different proposal relating to perpetual dynasty trusts, see Joint Committee on Taxation, *Options to Improve Tax Compliance and Reform Tax Expenditures* (JCS-02-05), January 27, 2005, pp. 392-95. The proposal generally prohibits the allocation of generation-skipping transfer tax exemption to a trust that can exist in perpetuity.

[134] Treas. Reg. sec. 1.1014-3(a).

[135] See Rev. Rul. 54-97, 1954-1 C.B. 113, 1954.

[136] See Technical Advice Memorandum 199933001, January 7, 1999. For property acquired by gift, the basis of the property in the hands of the donee generally is the same as it was in the hands of the donor. However, for the purpose of determining loss on subsequent sale, the basis of property in the hands of the donee is the lesser of the donor's basis or the fair market value of the property at the time of the gift. Sec. 1015(a).

[137] This preference is especially clear in the case of a spouse of the decedent. That spouse will not, for example, bear the burden of an estate tax on his or her bequest. Other beneficiaries generally will bear the burden of the estate tax and therefore may have competing preferences.

[138] Department of the Treasury, *General Explanations of the Administration's Fiscal Year 2016 Revenue Proposals,* February 2015, pp. 195-96.

[139] H.R. 1 (113th Cong., 2d Sess.), sec. 1422.

[140] Department of the Treasury, *General Explanations of the Administration's Fiscal Year 2016 Revenue Proposals,* February 2015, pp. 156-57.

[141] *Ibid.*

In: Federal Taxation of Wealth Transfers
Editor: Jerry Washington ISBN: 978-1-63482-991-5

Chapter 3

TESTIMONY OF RAY D. MADOFF, PROFESSOR OF LAW, BOSTON COLLEGE LAW SCHOOL. HEARING ON THE "BURDEN OF THE ESTATE TAX ON FAMILY BUSINESSES AND FARMS"*

Chairman Reichert, Ranking Member Neal, Members of the Subcommittee, thank you for inviting me to testify today and for holding this hearing. My testimony today will focus on (1) the importance of the estate tax, particularly in supporting the fairness of our tax system and (2) the significant societal costs that would result from repeal of the estate tax.

As an introductory matter, it is important to keep in mind that, in one form or another, the estate tax has been with us since this country's earliest days. The first estate tax was enacted in 1797, long before the income tax. Our modern estate tax was enacted in 1916, a mere three years after the enactment of the income tax.[2] Any tax that has stood the test of time for so long should not be repealed without due attention to the role that it plays in our society, and the negative repercussions that could result from its repeal.

* This is an edited, reformatted and augmented version of testimony presented March 18, 2015 before the House Ways and Means Committee, Subcommittee on Select Revenue Measures.

THE IMPORTANCE OF THE ESTATE TAX

The estate tax plays an essential role in our tax system because (1) it promotes fairness in the tax system; and (2) it provides an important source of revenue for the government.

Promoting Fairness. The estate tax promotes fairness by providing an essential counterweight to the extraordinary benefits conferred on inherited wealth under our income tax system. Our current income tax system favors inherited wealth in two significant ways:

First, inherited wealth is entirely excluded from income taxes. No matter how much wealth an individual inherits, whether it is $100, $100,000 or $100 million, she is treated the same for income tax purposes as a person who inherits nothing.[3] The failure to tax inherited wealth is particularly glaring in comparison to the taxes imposed on wages of working Americans, who are subject to income taxes of up to 39.6% and payroll taxes of up to 15.3%.

For example, a self-employed construction worker earning $60,000 a year building bridges, will owe federal income taxes of $7,159 and self-employment taxes of $8,468, resulting in a take home pay of only $44,363 (and for many taxpayers this will be further reduced by several thousand dollars of state income taxes.) By contrast, a person who inherits $60,000—even from a distant relative-- will enjoy the full $60,000 undiminished by taxes.[4] This decision to exclude inheritance from the income tax base while subjecting wages to taxes imposed at the highest tax rates, effectively shifts the tax burden from heirs to wage earners.

Second, those with inherited wealth enjoy special benefits with respect to taxation from sales of property. Normally, when an individual sells property, she is subject to tax on the difference between the amount she receives from the sale and the purchase price (called "basis"). If the property is passed on by gift, the recipient has the same basis in the property that the donor had (thus passing on any built-in gains to the recipient.) However, there is a special basis rule that applies to property passed on at death: in that case, the heir receives the property with a basis equal to the fair market value of the property at the time of the decedent's death (called "stepped-up basis.") The effect of stepped-up basis is that an heir can sell inherited property and pay no capital gains taxes, even if the decedent had significant untaxed built-in gains at the time of death.

Thus, if a decedent had invested $20,000 in Apple stock in the 1980's, and died in 2015 the stock would be worth well over $4 million at the time of death. But neither the decedent nor the decedent's heir would ever pay tax on that $4 million of gain since death is not a taxable event under the U.S. income tax law and the heir would receive the stock as if he had purchased it for its $4 million fair market value. Since this amount is less than the unified credit exemption amount for estate tax purposes, it is quite likely that this transfer will avoid estate taxes as well. Thus, the heir receives over $4 million tax-free and no one ever pays taxes on the $4 million of inherent capital gain.

This rule not only unfairly benefits heirs, but also interferes with the efficiency of the market by creating a lock-in effect. Owner are reluctant to sell capital assets because to do so would be to incur capital gains taxes that could be avoided simply by holding on to the property until death. If the owner needs access to funds during life, she can obtain that access in a tax-free way by simply borrowing against the assets. This ability to avoid capital gains taxes through borrowing is so well known that the simple advice to "buy, borrow and die" is referred to by one tax scholar as "Tax Planning 101."[5]

The preferential treatment of inherited wealth under the income tax system is often justified under the theory that property passed on at death is subject to estate taxes. Indeed, the relationship between the income tax benefits and the estate tax are so intertwined that if Congress were to repeal the estate tax, fairness would dictate that it should only do so only in conjunction with significantly restricting the benefits for inherited wealth provided under the income tax system.

Raising Revenue: In addition to promoting fairness, estate taxes provide an important source of revenue for the federal government. This revenue pays for valuable programs and allows the government to reduce the tax burden on other taxpayers. According to the most recent estimates, the estate tax will generate about $294 billion over the next 10 years. While this amount is small in relation to the amount raised by the income tax, it would still be enough to finance 100% of school nutrition programs which provide nutritious meals to 31 million children every day for 10 years; or it could finance free community college tuition for more than 9 million students over 10 years, 5 times over. Alternatively, these funds could be used to reduce corporate tax rates, which some say have put U.S. companies at a competitive disadvantage and encouraged some companies to go abroad.

One reason for the relatively small amount of income generated by the estate tax is legislative policy changes over the last decade that have eroded the value of the estate tax. Policies could be adopted to turn that trend the other way. First, the estate tax could be easily fortified by closing existing loopholes, especially those allowing manipulation of valuation. The decision to leave those loopholes in place reduces revenue and encourages taxpayers to game the system. The integrity of the system could easily be improved by making some simple changes to the Code. [6] Second, in recent years, Congress has acted to weaken the estate tax by steadily increasing the exemption amount and decreasing maximum tax rates.[7] This has significantly reduced the number of individuals subject to the estate tax as well as the amount of revenue generated by the tax.

If the estate tax were to be repealed, then, in order for repeal to be revenue neutral, the government would need to replace this foregone revenue by imposing a higher tax burden on other taxpayers. It's worth asking the where the lost revenue would come from. Would that revenue come from corporate tax increases? From individual tax increases? From excise tax increases? Additionally, any of these options would have to be examined in terms of their levels of progressivity (or regressivity) to ensure that tax burdens remain fair. Given that the estate tax is imposed on the wealthiest taxpayers, the impact of repeal would most likely result in shifting the tax burden down to those with fewer resources. If Congress were to choose to not to replace the revenue lost through repeal, we must question whether it is appropriate for Congress to add to the deficit in order to finance a major tax cut for the wealthy.

A Red Herring: Family Farms and Businesses

The strongest rhetorical argument in favor of repealing the estate tax is its potential impact on family farms and businesses. As a society, we value the idea of businesses staying within families. If the estate tax were to significantly limit that ability, then that could be a strong argument in favor of a legislative fix.

However, despite the rhetorical appeal of the family farm and business argument, it ultimately does not support estate tax repeal because (1) given the large exemption amount currently in effect (combined with the ability of spouses to combine their unified credit exemptions), the vast majority of family farms and businesses will fall within the exemption amount and therefore not be subject to the estate tax at all; (2) to the extent that a family farm or business is not covered by the $5/$10 million exemption there are statutory provisions designed to mitigate the impact of the estate tax; and (3) if Congress is still concerned about the potential impact of the estate tax on a family's ability to pass a family business on to the next generation, it need not repeal the estate tax, but rather could easily carve out a targeted exception that would exempt family farms and businesses from the estate tax.

Large Exemption Amount. Beginning in 2012 the estate tax exemption was increased to $5 million per person, adjusted for inflation. In 2015 each taxpayer can pass up to $5,430,000 free of estate taxes. Moreover, for married taxpayers the unified credits of both spouses can be combined, resulting in a married couple's ability to pass on well over $10 million of assets free of estate taxes. The vast majority of family businesses will fall well within this exemption amount.

Moreover, for family businesses that are larger than $10 million, the estate tax is only a problem if there are no other liquid assets with which to pay the tax. In many cases with estates of that size the beneficiaries will have enough other non-business assets with which to pay the estate tax liability.

Statutory Relief. For those businesses that are larger than $10 million and where there are insufficient non-business assets with which to pay the estate tax, there is statutory relief in the form of Section 6166 which permits the executor of an estate with a closely held business to pay estate taxes over a 15 year period, including paying only interest on the deferred tax for the first 5 years. Moreover, interest on these payments is generally charged at a below market basis. This provision allows for estate taxes to be paid over time out of the business's operating income.

A Targeted Benefit. If Congress wants to provide greater protections to family farms and businesses, it can do so by providing an outright exemption. This provision would be easy to draft because the statutory language was already drafted in connection with Section 2057, which provided an exclusion for a portion of a family farm or business passed on to family members. Although this provision was repealed in 2013 in connection with the overall increase in the estate tax exemption amount, it could easily be used as a template on which to fashion an exemption from estate taxes for farms and businesses being passed on to family members.

ANOTHER RED HERRING: THE ESTATE TAX DISCOURAGES HARD WORK

Proponents of repeal argue that estate taxes discourage hard work because it limits the ability of an individual to pass on property at death. However, this argument misconstrues the true beneficiaries of estate tax repeal. While repeal of the estate tax may provide some *emotional* benefit to those individuals who have earned wealth and want to pass it on to their heirs, the *financial* benefit of repeal flows entirely to the heirs of individuals passing on more than $5 million (or $10 million if married) of wealth. Rather than encouraging hard work, the failure to tax inherited wealth discourages hard work because it facilitates the creation of effortlessly wealthy heirs.

THE COST OF ESTATE TAX REPEAL

Repealing the estate tax would impose considerable burdens on society that go well beyond the loss of revenue that the estate tax raises. In particular: (1) repeal of the estate tax would cause even greater concentration of wealth among the wealthiest Americans, resulting in an aristocracy of wealth that threatens our most cherished democratic ideals and harms our economy; and (2) repeal of the estate tax could result in a significant reduction in charitable giving which would in turn have a devastating effect on the charitable sector and the people it serves.

Wealth Concentration. One thing we know for certain is that the repeal of the estate tax would result in greater concentration of wealth among heirs of wealthy individuals who, as a result of repeal, would receive greater inheritances because they would be undiminished by taxes. Moreover, through the use of dynasty trusts, this inherited wealth will be able to be protected from creditors and taxes in perpetuity. The combined effect of this will be to create an aristocracy of wealth based on birth that was just the type of thing that our forefathers tried to get away from in establishing the rules governing these United States.

Thomas Jefferson was particularly concerned about the effect of this type of aristocracy on democracy. As Jefferson wrote to John Adams on October 28th, 1813:

> For I agree with you that there is a natural aristocracy among men. The grounds of this are virtue and talents... There is also an artificial aristocracy founded on wealth and birth, without either virtue or talents; for with these it would belong to the first class. The natural aristocracy I consider as the most precious gift of nature for the instruction, the trusts, and government of society. And indeed it would have been inconsistent in creation to have formed man for the social state, and not to have provided virtue and wisdom enough to manage the concerns of the society. May we not even say that that form of government is the best which provides the most effectually for a pure selection of these natural aristoi into the

offices of government? The artificial aristocracy [i.e. that founded on wealth and birth] is a mischievous ingredient in government, and provision should be made to prevent its ascendancy.[8]

John Adams expressed this same concern when he wrote: "When economic power became concentrated in a few hands, then political power flowed to those possessors and away from the citizens, ultimately resulting in an oligarchy or tyranny."[9]

This same idea was reflected in the 20th century by Supreme Court Justice Louis Brandeis when he said: "We can have concentrated wealth in the hands of a few or we can have democracy. But we can't have both."[10]

Wealth concentration is also a problem from the point of view of the economic health of the country. As Nobel-prize winning economist Joseph Stiglitz has written: "Widely unequal societies do not function efficiently, and their economies are neither stable nor sustainable in the long term."[11] It should not be surprising that every empirical study that has examined the impact of inequality on long-term growth has shown that high concentrations of wealth correlate with poor economic performance.[12]

Finally, greater inequality of wealth has also been shown to correlate with other social problems including life expectancy, social mobility, rates of imprisonment and mental health. This correlation between wealth inequality and social problems exists regardless of the overall level of wealth in the country (that is, richer countries do not achieve better results if they have greater inequality.)[13]

Wealth concentration is not simply a product of an unfettered market, but rather is the product of government policies, including taxation, that allocate society's resources. For example, wealth concentration was significantly reduced in this country from the 1930's to the 1980's as a result of progressive estate and income tax rates, along with other policies designed to build a strong middle class (such as the G.I. bill, federal mortgage assistance programs and loans to small businesses). However, beginning in the 1980s, and accelerating through the early part of this century, this trend reversed and wealth concentration again became a prominent feature of our economic landscape.[14]

A recent paper by Emmanuel Saez and Gabriel Zucman tracking wealth distribution from 1913-2012 quantifies this trend (graphs attached as Appendix A).[15] This paper shows how, over the past century the wealth of the wealthiest 0.1% of Americans has followed a U-shaped pattern: in the roaring 20's the wealthiest Americans controlled 25% of the country's wealth. By the mid-1970s (with the growth of the middle class), the wealthiest owned only 7% of the country's wealth. However, since then, the concentration of wealth among the wealthiest Americans has increased and today the wealthiest 0.1% of the population (those families with $20 million or more) own 22% of the country's wealth.

During this same period, the wealth of the remaining 90% of the population has followed the opposite trend. From the mid-1920's to the mid-1980's there was a great democratization of wealth and the amount of wealth owned by 90% of the population went from 15% to 36%. However, since then the amount of wealth owned by 90% of the country has fallen dramatically to 23%.

We are now coming close to full circle in terms of wealth inequality. Today, the wealthiest 0.1% of Americans own roughly the same amount of wealth as that which is owned by 90% of the population. Repeal of the estate tax would further accelerate this alarming trend.

Charitable Giving. The charitable sector plays a central role in the United States. Unlike many other countries that finance education, health care, scientific research, arts, and social safety nets primarily through direct government expenditures, the United States supports these important activities largely through private donations subsidized indirectly by the government through tax deductions for charitable giving. As such, society is deeply dependent on charitable giving, even more so in a world where vital national interests are forced to compete for scarce government resources.

The estate tax charitable deduction plays an important role in encouraging charitable giving. Unlike the income tax deduction, which is limited to no more than 50% of a donor's income, the estate tax provides an unlimited charitable deduction that allows all individuals subject to the estate tax to essentially opt out of the tax by committing their resources to charitable ends. Many estates take advantage of this such that over 8% of all charitable giving is in the form of bequests at death. In addition, much lifetime giving is likely motivated by estate tax savings as well, as property transferred to a charity during life is also exempt under the gift and estate tax system.

The estate tax charitable deduction has been with us since the inception of the estate tax almost 100 years ago. Therefore, it is very difficult to predict the effect of repeal on charitable giving. However, given our reliance on the charitable sector to provide our most essential services, even a small reduction in charitable giving arising from repeal could prove devastating for the sector and the individuals that it serves.

Conclusion

Thank you again for inviting me to testify today. I hope that my perspective on these issues helps the Committee as it thinks about whether to repeal the estate tax.

Appendix A

This figure depicts the share of total household wealth held by the 0.1% richest families, as estimated by capitalizing income tax returns. In 2012, the top 0.1% includes about 160,000 families with net wealth above $20.6 million. Source: Appendix Table B1.

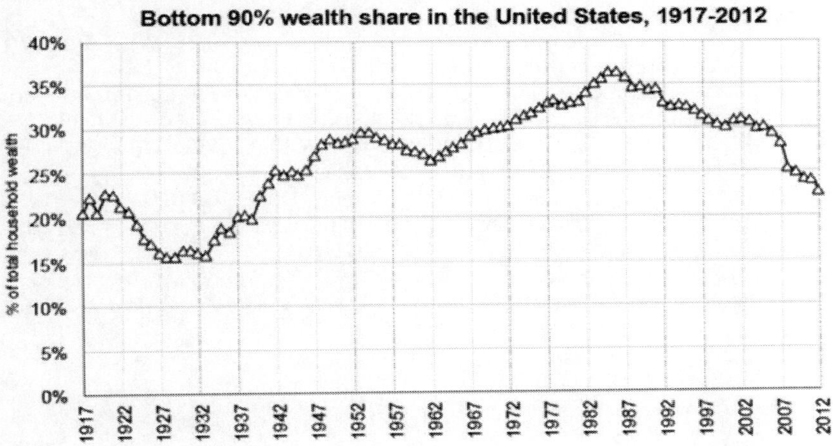

End Notes

[1] Professor of Law, Boston College Law School.

[2] The history of the wealth transfer tax system is described in: STAFF OF JOINT COMM. ON TAXATION, HISTORY, PRESENT LAW, AND ANALYSIS OF THE WEALTH TRANSFER TAX SYSTEM, JCX-108-07, at 1-10 (2007).

[3] I.R.C. § 102 (2015). This rule also applies to property received by gift and through life insurance.

[4] The argument that inherited wealth has already been subject to income taxes when earned by the decedent is in most cases false and in any event irrelevant. First, most inherited wealth is in the form of capital assets and, as explained in the text, capital gains evade taxation when passed on at death. Second, even if some income had been taxed when earned by the decedent, that does not mean that it should avoid taxation when received by the heir. Taxes are imposed on individuals, not on dollars. Therefore, the fact that money was taxed when acquired by one person has no bearing on whether it should be taxed when acquired by another. When a person uses post-tax income to hire a mechanic to fix his car, the mechanic cannot avoid taxation on that income on the grounds that the funds have already been subject to tax. Finally, even single individuals are commonly subject to multiple types of taxes on the same money. Wages are subject to income and payroll taxes and if those post-tax funds are used to purchase houses and cars, they are then subject to sales taxes and property taxes. There is no recognized tax policy against multiple types of taxes being imposed on the same funds.

[5] Edward J. McCaffery, Distracted from Distraction by Distraction: Reimagining Estate Tax Reform, 40 PEPPERDINE LAW REVIEW 1235, 1250 (2013).

[6] James R. Repetti, Revitializing the Estate Tax: Five Easy Pieces, 142 TAX NOTES 1231 (2014).

[7] RAY D. MADOFF, CORNELIA R. TENNEY, MARTIN A. HALL & LISA N. MINGOLLA, PRACTICAL GUIDE TO ESTATE PLANNING §5.04 (2015).

[8] http://press-pubs.uchicago.edu/founders/documents/v1ch15s61.html

[9] WILLIAM H. GATES & CHUCK COLLINS, WEALTH AND OUR COMMONWEALTH: WHY AMERICA SHOULD TAX ACCUMULATED FORTUNES 29 (2004).

[10] Ibid., p. 17.

[11] JOSEPH E. STIGLITZ, THE PRICE OF INEQUALITY: HOW TODAY'S DIVIDED SOCIETY ENDANGERS OUR FUTURE 83 (2013).

[12] Paul Caron and James R. Repetti, Occupy the Tax Code: Using the Estate Tax to Reduce Inequality and Spur Economic Growth, 40 PEPPERDINE LAW REVIEW 1255 (2012)

[13] RICHARD WILKINSON AND KATE PICKET, THE SPIRIT LEVEL: WHY GREATER EQUALITY MAKES SOCIETIES STRONGER (2009).

[14] GATES & COLLINS, supra note 9, at 15; EDWARD B. WOLFF, TOP HEAVY: A STUDY OF THE INCREASING INEQUALITY OF WEALTH IN AMERICA, 8-13 (1995).

[15] Emmanuel Saez & Gabriel Zucman, Wealth Inequality in the United States since 1913: Evidence from Capital Income Tax Data (Nat'l Bureau of Econ. Research, Working Paper No. 20625, 2014), available at http://gabrielzucman.eu/files/SaezZucman2014.pdf.

In: Federal Taxation of Wealth Transfers
Editor: Jerry Washington
ISBN: 978-1-63482-991-5

Chapter 4

STATEMENT OF BRANDON WHITT, BATEY FARMS. HEARING ON THE "BURDEN OF THE ESTATE TAX ON FAMILY BUSINESSES AND FARMS"*

Chairman Reichert, Ranking Member Neal and members of the Subcommittee. My name is Brandon Whitt. I am a 7th generation farmer from Murfeesboro, Tennessee, where I farm with my wife, Katherine, and father-in-law, John, in a suburbanized area just outside of Nashville. Batey Farms dates back to 1807, beginning from a revolutionary war land grant for military service. Over its 208 years, the farm has seen many faces, developments, victories and failures but one thing remains constant, we strive to uphold the principle of our family motto "preserving the past and embracing the future."

Batey Farms is very diverse and includes a market that sells the fruits, vegetables and pork we produce directly to consumers. In addition, we farm 1,800 acres of row crops and 250 acres of hay on our own land and land we rent from neighboring landowners. My wife and I manage the day-to-day operation of our farm business while my father-in-law, who still works daily alongside me, owns the land we farm. We employ one full time, two part time and a dozen seasonal workers. Over 65,000 customers pass through our farm gate annually and we are currently investing to expand our agri-tourism attractions so that more of our urban neighbors will visit and make a connection to modern day agriculture.

* This is an edited, reformatted and augmented version of a statement presented March 18, 2015 before the House Ways and Means Committee, Subcommittee on Select Revenue Measures.

When my wife's grandmother passed in 1988, my father-in-law, who had farmed the land his entire life, was faced with a huge estate tax. The farm at the time was a little over 600 acres. Land values were booming and the value of the farm had doubled over the previous 10 years. John ended up having to sell 120 acres of land to pay estate taxes. This may not sound like much of a sacrifice since it left him with 483 acres to farm, but it completely changed the farm business. The land was lost to development and having houses so close to our fields made it impossible for us to continue raising cattle.

Fast forward to today: we still farm that same land, only now it is easily valued at $25,000 per acre. Some might say that we should sell out and start over somewhere else, but this is not my family's plan. We believe that Batey Farms will be a viable farm business far into the future and we hope that our children will be the 8th generation to farm our land. We believe that our farm adds value to our town, that our neighbors value our open space, that our customers value having a local food source and that our farm market creates a sense of community. We intend to honor our motto and continue our farming business as long as we are able.

My father-in-law John is now 72 years old. As we look to the future, we can't help but worry about what will happen when he passes away. We have spent countless hours talking with financial advisors, accountants and attorneys trying to put together a plan that will allow Batey Farms to remain a viable business. We know that we will face an estate tax when my father-in-law dies and we are planning now to try to avoid having to sell more acres to pay the tax. I can't help but think about what our farm might be like if we could have invested all that time and energy into our business.

My story is the story of young farmers all over the country. Agriculture looks different on farms from state to state but we all face the same reality that an uncertain tomorrow can bring. We face decisions about making long-term investments in our farms and ranches without the benefit of knowing the price we will be paid for our products. We deal with unpredictable weather that can change a good year into a bad one with a single storm. There isn't much we can do about these risks. They are a normal part of the uncertainty that goes along with farming. But why should uncertainties over estate taxes be added to these others? Our job is hard enough as it is.

I urge Congress to abolish the federal estate tax so that farms like mine can better use their resources to build a stronger business and better their communities. I urge Congress to act quickly to end estate taxes so that no other farmer or rancher has to sell part of his or her business to pay this misguided tax.

In: Federal Taxation of Wealth Transfers
Editor: Jerry Washington
ISBN: 978-1-63482-991-5

Chapter 5

TESTIMONY OF ROBERT E. MCKNIGHT, MCKNIGHT RANCH CO. HEARING ON THE "BURDEN OF THE ESTATE TAX ON FAMILY BUSINESSES AND FARMS"*

Dear Chairman Reichert and Ranking Member Neal:

My name is Bobby McKnight and I am a seventh-generation cattleman from Fort Davis, Texas. It is my privilege to appear before this committee today and speak on behalf of cattlemen and women across America and discuss an uncomfortable issue that too many of us have faced the death tax. I am here to share my story so that you can have a better understanding of the personal impact the death tax has on hard-working American families like mine. Having dealt with the death tax on multiple occasions, I can assure you that it s not easy to have the burden of settling the estate of a loved one while coping with the loss of that loved one. To add insult to injury, it is even more stressful when you discover that the estate you are trying to settle is subject to the federal death tax. How will I pay the estate tax? Will I have to sell off part of my business or take out a loan to pay this tax? Will I be forced to lay off employees? These are all questions that I have had to face on multiple occasions. My story, unfortunately, is not that uncommon among the cattle families of this great nation.

---

* This is an edited, reformatted and augmented version of testimony presented March 18, 2015 before the House Ways and Means Committee, Subcommittee on Select Revenue Measures.

As a cattleman, the most important part of my family s livelihood is the health and safety of my cattle. Every day, I get up and work along-side my employees because every hand in the operation has the responsibility to look after the cattle and put the needs of the cattle above our own. I worry about if they are getting enough food and water. I look after them and fight off predators and keep disease away from the herd. Cattle don t take a day off, so neither can I. I am financially and emotionally invested in the success of the herd. It is my duty to take care of these animals and the people who work for me.

My ranch is a family-owned small business. Sometimes I need up to seven employees to help me run my operation efficiently. Over the years I have invested a lot of time, resources, and sweat equity in developing my employees. We work along-side each other taking care of the livestock and hoping for a good year where we will all reap the benefits of hard work. When times have been lean I have had to make sacrifices to keep my business above water and to keep my employees on the ranch. I make it a priority to put our people first because I don t want to let them go. But sometimes you run out of places to cut and you have to make the uncomfortable decision to cut seasoned employees. That is what happened to my family during hard times brought on by the estate tax. At one time I had to cut my staff by sixty-five percent. I had to let go of seasoned employees that had families of their own and they were forced to find work elsewhere. The skill set needed to work cattle is a special skill set that takes years to learn, and I would give anything to have that skilled labor back working for me once more.

Like other small businesses I have to worry about making payroll, complying with numerous federal and state regulations, and paying bills, loans, and taxes in full and on time. I face the same stresses that other small business owner's face, all the while praying that the drought will end and I won't face another summer of devastating wildfires. My cattle need good pasture and plenty of water to thrive, but the wildfires and drought have been a heavy burden on ranchers like me all across the Southwestern United States. Many of my neighbors worry about whether they can make it through another dry year without being forced to sell their herds and their businesses. That is a lot of stress for any business owner to handle. Now add to that the onerous compliance of the death tax.

I am a member of the National Cattlemen's Beef Association (NCBA), the largest and oldest national association of cattle producers. NCBA has represented America's cattlemen and women since 1898, preserving the heritage and strength of the cattle industry through education and public policy. As the largest and oldest national association of cattle producers, NCBA represents a very diverse beef industry that strives to meet demand in emerging markets and increase demand for beef. Repealing the death tax is a top priority for NCBA, and without question, we offer our utmost support in repealing the death tax.

When most people think of the cattle industry, they think of my home state of Texas. While Texas is one of the largest beef-producing states, the U.S. beef industry is very diverse with production in all fifty states including Alaska and Hawaii. One common fear facing America's beef-producing families is the uncertainty of and compliance with the death tax. In fact, the death tax is considered one of the leading causes of the breakup of multi-generation family farms and ranches.

As you probably know, many farm and ranch families are asset-rich and cash-poor, with most of the value of their estate attributed to the value of the land they use to raise cattle and grow food and fiber for consumers around the world. The agriculture industry has enjoyed a successful run over the past few years with strong foreign demand for U.S. agricultural goods. Strong export demand has been one of the driving forces in the increase in value of crop land and pasture land in almost every state. Not to mention the pressure from commercial developers who also want to purchase the land. Combined together, the increase in value of farmland has many farm and ranch families concerned that they may trigger the estate tax simply through increasing land values.

Some people make the mistake in thinking that livestock operations that own a lot of land must be wealthy and can afford to pay more in taxes. Keep in mind that beef production in the United States varies from state to state. For instance, in the Southeastern United States most herds are smaller and need fewer acres to be successful because they have good pastures that receive a lot of rain. On the other hand, where I live the annual rainfall average is less than eighteen inches so we need more acres to support the same number of cattle. Likewise, some people make the mistake of equating large herds with large profits. Cows need plenty of food and water to grow to the desired adult weight. The more cows you have, the higher your input costs will be. And given the market volatility in the price of cattle feed, hay, water and fuel, profit margins can be small for large herds and they face a greater risk of loss. Plus, not all animals will receive the same price when harvested. The price received for each cow depends on the quality of the product, not the quantity. When it comes down to it, the pain is felt by all operations no matter the herd size.

Simply put, in an industry as diverse as ours it is easy to mistake size of the operation with the success of the operation.

The uncertainty of the tax code has made it difficult for many farmers and ranchers to establish long-term business plans. This is especially frustrating when your business already faces unpredictable factors like the price of inputs and the weather. The truth is it is very hard to predict whether or not an operation will be successful this year or the next. The market value of cattle fluctuates, as do the costs of inputs like feed, water, and fuel, plus the fact that the cattle industry is not subsidized by the federal government.

At the end of 2012, Congress passed the American Taxpayer Relief Act (ATRA) narrowly avoiding a return to a $1 million estate tax exemption with a 55 percent tax rate by setting the estate tax exemption level at $5 million per individual ($10 million per couple) and the top tax rate to 40 percent. ATRA also maintained the spousal transfer, the step-up in basis and indexes the estate tax for inflation. While not perfect, ATRA provided relief for some producers but unfortunately the estate tax still impacts family farmers and ranchers across the United States and it must be repealed.

Even with ATRA, many farm and ranch families must still invest time and resources into planning and complying with the estate tax. For those of us who put together an estate plan, we must continue to spend money on lawyers and accountants to make sure that plan is compliant with the law. But what about those who do not have an estate plan? What if the death in the family was sudden and unexpected and they could not have planned for it? How much will they have to spend on lawyers and accountants? Unfortunately, all too often at the time of death, farming and ranching families are forced to lay off employees, sell off land, farm equipment, parts of the operation or the entire ranch to pay off tax liabilities. Even with an estate plan it can take years to transfer assets which will incur unanticipated costs to the family—implementing asset transfer it is not free. In most cases, these assets have already been taxed at the federal, state, and local levels many times over the course of a lifetime.

As someone who has been on the negative end of the death tax, I would like to know what, if any, are the positive benefits of the death tax? When faced with the death tax I am no longer thinking about how I can grow my business and hire more employees. No, I am focused on whether I need to liquidate assets to control loss. I would rather focus on expanding my herd and re-investing in my community by creating jobs. I would like to know if the Government of the United States is more interested in farmers and ranchers spending time and money on complying with the death tax or creating more jobs.

Some in Washington may see the death tax as a minor inconvenience for the wealthy, something that does not deserve attention. The truth is, when the death tax lands on your doorstep, it is a very big deal. The death tax impacts more than just the family, it affects the employees of the impacted business and the other local businesses who are losing customers. The death tax has a ripple effect that impacts local economies for many years and many times the damage cannot be undone. This is not a tax on the wealthy elite in America. It's a death warrant for far too many family businesses.

For decades, NCBA has fought for full and permanent repeal of the estate tax and we will continue to do so until permanent repeal is achieved. NCBA strongly supports the *Death Tax Repeal Act of 2015* and we urge all Members of Congress to support the full and final repeal of the death tax. I thank you for this opportunity and hope my comments have shed light on the truth about the death tax.

Sincerely,
Robert E. McKnight
Fort Davis, Texas

In: Federal Taxation of Wealth Transfers
Editor: Jerry Washington
ISBN: 978-1-63482-991-5

Chapter 6

TESTIMONY OF KAREN MADONIA, CHIEF FINANCIAL OFFICER, ILLCO, INC. HEARING ON THE "BURDEN OF THE ESTATE TAX ON FAMILY BUSINESSES AND FARMS"*

Chairman Reichert, Ranking Member Neal and Members of the Subcommittee on Select Revenue Measures, my name is Karen Madonia, and I am the Chief Financial Officer and next generation of Illco, Inc., a Chicago-area distributor of heating, ventilation, air-conditioning and refrigeration equipment, parts and supplies. Thank you for giving me the opportunity to talk about the estate tax and its effect on the many small family businesses that comprise the United States economy. This is an issue that is very close to my heart as my family is in the midst of our own generational transfer.

Let me provide you with some background: Illco was a very small company with only seven employees when my father purchased it back in 1973. At that time, my dad was only 32 years old, with a wife, three daughters and a mortgage, but he knew he wanted something more than just a job. He wanted to use his passion to create something permanent, to be in control of his own destiny. With help from my grandfather, my dad decided to take a risk and go into business for himself. A community bank took my grandfather's assets, my dad's assets and a guarantee from a vendor as collateral for a $340,000 loan to purchase the company.

* This is an edited, reformatted and augmented version of testimony presented March 18, 2015 before the House Ways and Means Committee, Subcommittee on Select Revenue Measures.

In those early years, my dad worked every job at Illco. During the day, he went to see customers and secure orders, then went back to the warehouse to pull and package them. The next day, he would make deliveries using my mom's station wagon before visiting more customers and taking more orders. Eventually, he was able to buy a truck and hire a driver, which left the station wagon free for my mom to pick up merchandise from Illco vendors while my sisters and I were at school. After the doors closed at 5:00, my dad would go to his office to perform both the accounts payable and accounts receivable functions. Every bit of profit he made got funneled back into the company so he could hire more people, buy more trucks and expand his inventory. My dad worked seven days a week, and most nights he did not get home until long after most people had finished their dinners. He had to give up any hobbies which took too much time away from his business, and our family vacations were mostly extended weekends because a week was simply too long for him to be away. Many weekends were spent entertaining customers, mostly over home-cooked meals, because that was the only way my parents could afford to wine and dine the people that were so necessary to the success of the business. But my dad's passion for the industry, his commitment to his employees, and his drive to grow his company empowered him to keep pushing even when interest rates hovered in the high teens during the late 1970's and early 1980's and things looked pretty ominous. Forty years later, he has a business with eight branches in three states, 97 employees and $42,000,000 in revenue.

My sisters and I grew up understanding that if we wanted to be successful at anything, we had to work hard and stay focused on our goals. We are all proud to work alongside our dad now, and look forward to making our own mark on the family business in the coming years. There is also a generation behind us that is just beginning to consider career options. Perhaps some of them will join usÉthat is certainly my hope. But after years of listening to us struggle to figure out how to grow the business while navigating the estate tax waters, I imagine that all of them will think twice before making that leap.

For the last few years, I have come to Washington with our trade association, HARDI, to talk to Members of the House and Senate about the issues that are important to our companies and our industry. Every year, estate tax is on the top of my list of topics to discuss. I personally find it fundamentally wrong to place a tax on death. If a person accumulates wealth through hard work, and if that person pays his fair share of taxes on income as it is earned, I do not understand how the government can justify taking a significant portion of what he has left simply because he opted to save and re-invest rather than consume. The United States has already benefited from that person's success because he has employed people who pay taxes, bought buildings on which he has paid property taxes and bought inventory and supplies from other companies, which can then afford to employ more people who pay taxes. He has created opportunity for the community as a whole while creating prosperity for himself. We all benefit when a small businessperson succeeds. To me, and probably to a large portion of the generation behind me, the estate tax serves as a tremendous entrepreneurial disincentive. Why work hard to build something substantial if it is likely to die when you do? Why not be just another worker, make enough money to live comfortably, and not worry about generating any more wealth than that? If even a small percentage of potential entrepreneurs decide not to turn their dreams into viable businesses because our tax policy discourages them from doing so, haven't we done a great disservice to our economy?

Proponents of the estate tax will tell you tell it prevents the concentrated accumulation of wealth in our country. They'll tell you that our nation needs to increase taxes on the "wealthy" because they need to pay their "fair share". On the surface, that's a pretty safe argument to make. It's easy to say the solution to our fiscal issues is to increase the burden on those who can afford it the most. But what's fair about paying taxes your whole life only to have to pay even more at death simply because you're leaving a business behind? What is always overlooked in these discussions is the effect of the estate tax on the small family business. In most cases, we're not talking about passing on bank accounts with multi-million dollar balances. We're talking about businesses where most of the net worth is tied up in inventory, accounts receivable, equipment and real estate. At Illco, for example, we carry an inventory valued at $12,000,000 and accounts receivable of about $5,000,000. Our inventory has to be high – we provide vital heating, air-conditioning and refrigeration parts and supplies to hospitals, schools, nursing homes and grocery stores. When the refrigeration system in a grocery store goes down, it needs to be repaired within hours or the food is lost. When the air conditioning system in a hospital doesn't work, patients cannot be appropriately cared for until air is circulating again. The parts and supplies that we sell must be on hand in order to facilitate quick repairs and replacements, which means that we must carry a heavy inventory. We also own five buildings and operate a fleet of twenty-four trucks, some of which cost upwards of $250,000. After paying our taxes and making our annual profit sharing contribution to our employees, the income that's left is put right back into the company so we can continue to carry an extensive inventory, extend payment terms to our customers and maintain our fleet and our buildings. If something happened to my dad and we were left with a large estate tax bill, we would literally have to sell parts of the company in order to pay it. That would likely mean shutting down branches, laying off workers or liquidating inventory just to be able to pay a tax bill that only occurred because an owner died. Even worse, our company might have to be sold outright, which would likely mean that instead of our employees being part of our small business family, they would become part of a larger company that is beholden to Wall Street. That would not benefit them, and I would argue that it wouldn't benefit the economy as a whole either. Small businesses employ over half of the nation's private sector workforce and create the vast majority of new jobs. With our economy in a relatively slow recovery, government should be encouraging us to grow and prosper. Instead, worry over the estate tax forces us to spend too much time and money focusing on things that have nothing to do with our businesses.

Over the last few years, my dad has spent countless hours and entirely too much money trying to figure out how his company can outlive him. Instead of focusing on growing his business so he can open more branches and employ more people, he has had to strategize about how to pass his company on to his kids without having to dismantle it. Most of our strategic management decisions, whether they are about day-to-day operations or opportunities to expand, involve consideration of the estate tax in one way or another. We have opted to maintain a large cash reserve as a precaution. Other companies choose to protect themselves by purchasing insurance. Either way, money that could be used to grow and create jobs is sitting on the sidelines. The estate tax is a huge roadblock to successful family businesses undergoing generational transfers. Think about thatÉperhaps the greatest challenge in transitioning a business from one generation to the next is our own tax code.

The United States has always been the land of opportunity. Small business owners take tremendous risk at great personal sacrifice, and they truly are the backbone of the American economy. No one is asking for it to be easy. In fact, my dad would probably be the first to tell you that working to overcome the challenges is the most rewarding part of owning your own business. But it shouldn't be the case that the thing that keeps you up at night is the worry that you may leave your kids with a huge tax burden when you die. I believe that most people would be proponents of an overhaul to our tax code. There probably are too many exemptions and loopholes that only upper income people can take advantage of, and those topics are worthy of a national conversation. But taxing the estates of successful entrepreneurs is punitive, and that is not the role that our tax code should play.

Two years ago, when Congress last addressed the issue of the estate tax, you gave the small business community some certainty by establishing an exemption and indexing it to inflation. While we still maintained that full repeal was the right answer, we appreciated that you understood that changing the rules on us every year made it impossible for us to properly plan for the future of our businesses. I respectfully ask that you again carefully consider all the ramifications of estate tax policy and then vote, once and for all, to permanently repeal the estate tax. Let's encourage families to create wealth by starting their own businesses, not threaten to take it away from them if the government thinks they have accumulated too much. Let's unleash the potential of those citizens willing to work hard and create something that will benefit all of us, not discourage their ambition through our tax code.

Thank you for the opportunity to share my family story with you. I would be happy to answer any questions that you may have.

INDEX

G

H

I

J

L

S

T

U

V

W